Turning Projects

Turning Projects

Richard Raffan

The Taunton Press

Front-cover photos by Susan Kahn
Front-cover inset photo by John Kelsey
Back-cover inset photo by Charley Robinson

...by fellow enthusiasts

First printing: January 1991
Printed in the United States of America

A FINE WOODWORKING Book

FINE WOODWORKING® is a trademark of The Taunton Press, Inc.
registered in the U.S. Patent and Trademark Office.

The Taunton Press
63 South Main Street
Box 5506
Newtown, CT 06470-5506

Library of Congress Cataloging-in-Publication Data

Raffan, Richard.
    Turning projects / Richard Raffan.
        p.   cm.
    "A Fine woodworking book" — T.p. verso.
        Includes index.
        ISBN 0-942391-38-1 : $19.95
    1. Turning.   I. Title.
TT201.R338   1990   90-49026
674'.8—dc20   CIP

Contents

Introduction

Turning a lump of wood spinning on a lathe can provide some of life's more satisfying and sensual experiences, as well as being just good plain fun. As streamers of curly shavings and smooth, flowing forms emerge as if by magic, you can make yourself all kinds of useful or utterly frivolous bits and pieces.

When I began to turn wood in 1970, I had no experience of the craft. But by making many of the designs included here by the hundred, and often thousand, I developed most of my basic technical skills. I often wonder what has happened to all those knobs, scoops, rollers, bashers, boards and trays that paid the bills during my early years at the lathe before market demand enabled me to concentrate on, and survive by, making bowls. Only rarely do I return to such batch production, but on each occasion I continue to find it pleasurable. And although it might not be quite as profitable financially as turning bowls, it further refines my technical skills.

Some of the projects in this book, such as the spurtle, are simple. Projects such as the hollow vessel, hand mirror and long, thin spindle demand more technique and precision. For contrast, I have included a carver's mallet and rodents (yes, rodents, as in mice) whose basic forms allow you to enjoy the shavings while you develop confidence at the lathe. Turning should be stimulating, occasionally challenging and, above all, an enjoyable way of passing the time, be it for profit or relaxation.

Until the craft revival of the 1970s, the lathe remained primarily a tool for the rapid production of treen or, more usually, components to be used elsewhere in the woodworking industries. Traditionally, apprentices learned the trade by undertaking small repetitious jobs, such as simple spindles for chairs or tool handles; here they would waste little material while still contributing to production. But few amateur turners want to cope with the volume of such production or the eventual monotony. Rare is a man I met in New Zealand a few years back, who developed his basic technique while turning several hundred spindles for the balcony running around three sides of his house. The spindles on the east side, turned first, show heaps of ineptitude with the tools — their diameters vary, squashed beads are legion and heavy sanding both distorted detailing and created deep score marks. These spindles contrast dramatically with the later ones, which show a growing mastery of the tools and feature even beads and consistent diameters. To some eyes the balcony might appear an uneven hotchpotch, but for me the complete set of spindles stands as a monument to determination and perseverance.

Constant repetition is undoubtedly the only way to gain true competence. If you want to earn a living by turning wood, you will benefit from making hundreds of each project, as I did. Along the way you'll really develop a feel for the material and forms, as well as the speed essential to competitive pricing, and thus survival. Clearly, hobby turners won't want all that production cluttering up the house. But by completing only a few versions of each project, you'll develop overall proficiency and assemble some nice pieces to enhance not only your own day-to-day life, but also the lives of the friends and relatives for whom you turn gifts.

Or maybe you'll run out of storage space and have to start selling. If you do choose to market what you make, try to develop your own detailing, which will make the work truly yours rather than a copy of something you see within these covers. This book should serve as a starting point from which your individual style will emerge. Every time you seek to repeat one particular detail or feature in favor of another, you'll move farther along your own stylistic path. Follow your design inclinations first, and make your judgments later. You might even want to join one of the hundreds of local woodturning groups for mutual assessment or reassurance. It always helps to view one object in relation to another, rather than in isolation.

This book does not dwell on turning technique or tools, since I wrote at length on those topics in *Turning Wood with Richard Raffan* (The Taunton Press, Newtown, Conn., 1985). I have, however, included observations and insights into the tools and techniques that have occurred to me during the intervening years between that book (and my second one, *Turned-Bowl Design,* published by The Taunton Press in 1987) and this one. The projects need not be tackled in order, since each is selected primarily to show how the various aspects of turning combine as work proceeds, as well as ways to approach typical problems. Some projects are intended to teach one skill or technique, and I refer you back to these from other parts of the book as necessary. For example, you might experience difficulty cutting grooves on the meat-mallet head or making the entry cut on a tray. In each case, I refer you to bead turning (pp. 54-63) to remind you about pivotal grips.

Sizes for the project blanks are not intended to be mandatory, and metric measurements frequently are rounded to the nearest 5mm for convenience. I rarely mention the wood used because I feel that it's too easy to become preoccupied with the material. All wood will look much the same in a few decades, if not sooner, so I prefer to concentrate on form and proportion. Grain patterns and color are mostly useful at the point and time of sale. When possible, I focus on the quality of material you should choose or avoid for a particular job. Grain and quality can vary wildly in one tree, let alone across a species.

I finish these projects with a simple oil-and-wax treatment applied as the lathe is running. First, I hold a rag soaked in mineral oil or vegetable oil against the sanded surface, then a lump of soft beeswax, which leaves a layer of wax over the oil. Finally, I firmly apply a soft cloth—in a few seconds, the wax melts and mixes with the oil for a soft matte finish that can be polished or washed, depending on the nature of the piece and its guardian.

Notes on Approach

If you are serious about developing your turning skills, always use the techniques that yield the best results directly, even though they might involve considerable risk to the job at first. An easy solution that requires little dexterity doesn't necessarily lead to the best results. Although you can carve out just about any shape using abrasives, my aim is to help you achieve the surface you want where you want it, quickly and efficiently and with minimal sanding.

Always attempt to reduce to a minimum the pressure that the rotating wood exerts against a tool edge. The constant in this situation is the rotating wood; the variable is the force with which you push the tool against the wood. In this life, if you meet force directly with force, you will always have conflict. So come sneaking in from an angle and use the energy to your advantage. When turning wood, aim to keep the tool bevel just rubbing against the wood rather than pushing against it. *The fact that any possibility of fine tool control vanishes if you force the tool into the wood cannot be stated often enough.*

Always allow a margin for error, by doing only what is necessary at a given stage. For instance, when making the outside of a tray, you finish the base, but not the sides. There's no point in wasting time and material completing the sides when they'll probably need skimming true because the partly turned job didn't center accurately when rechucked. Remember that even the skilled practitioners of a craft don't do everything right all the time. The vagaries of material and life will usually ensure that perfection remains a rare, if not unattainable, event.

Always err on the side of caution when setting lathe speeds, rather than risking danger with an "it'll be all right" attitude. Mostly it might be all right, but you need only one blank to fly off to lose an eye or half your teeth. Always stand clear of the path blanks will take if they do fly off. Wear eye protection or (preferably) a face shield.

Constant searching for tools and equipment is a ridiculously inefficient use of time and effort, so endeavor to impose order upon your work. Everything should have its place when not in use, so that you know where to find it when you need it. Throw worn abrasives out, and keep the rest in neat piles sorted according to grit. A daily cleanup is essential, not just to control dust and mess, but to limit fire hazards. I find a small mobile dust collector is essential at the source, collecting dust straight from the tools and abrasives. It's also a great aid to vacuuming at the end of the day, and it's good for the car, too.

Finally, craftsmanship is more about knowing what to do when things go wrong or, even more important, about anticipating hazards and overcoming them before a problem develops. The greater your experience, the more information you'll have on which to base your actions. And we're back to the benefits of repetition again.

1.Centerwork

Many turners concentrate on making bowls or other facework projects. They are drawn, I suspect, by the glamour of the grain patterns, which are typically more spectacular than on centerwork projects. Other turners discover that they encounter fewer difficulties when turning bowls or platters than when turning centerwork projects. All this is a great pity, because I find that most of the real challenges of turning wood, and the consequent satisfaction when these challenges are surmounted, come from working between centers.

Centerwork means that the grain of the wood runs parallel to the lathe axis, not merely that the wood is fixed between two centers. To obtain a clean surface efficiently and enjoyably, the wood has to be shear-cut (see the bottom drawing on p. 7). Using scraping techniques on centerwork projects generally will tear the fibers of the wood disastrously. This fact probably gave birth to the myth that real turners never use scrapers. But although real centerwork turners never use scrapers, real facework turners frequently do, as when turning into end grain (see Chapters 2 and 3).

Without a doubt, skew chisels are the best tools for centerwork. They're also more difficult to master than gouges and commonly associated with monumental catches capable of messing up your beads or even destroying the job. I find students are apprehensive—even scared—of the skew, knowing that a catch is always lurking. Hoping to avoid the frustrations of a catch ruining their work as it nears completion, most opt for the less efficient gouges or scrapers, only to end up with a second-rate job. Those who persevere and eventually come to grips with the skew discover in the process that their new skills make bowl turning ridiculously easy and in fact enhance all other aspects of turning. Time spent learning the skew is time spent mastering basic turning technique. You will reap huge benefits later.

The number of catches you experience using the skew should diminish greatly once you understand the dynamics of a catch. It all has to do with controlling the leverage. As shown in the top left drawing on the facing page, the skew contacts the rest at A, which is the fulcrum, with the side B raised off the rest. The wood rotating against the cutting edge at C exerts pressure against the tool. It is essential to keep this pressure on the far side of the fulcrum (at A) so that you can equalize the pressure on your side of the fulcrum (which is the handle). If the point of cut drifts toward D and your side of the fulcrum, point A actually becomes a hinge. The pressure of the wood makes the tool flutter, but this is merely a prelude to the main event, which is the point digging in. This snaps side B down onto the rest, kicking the tool slightly sideways to create those really big spiral dig-ins. The top right drawing shows the skew chisel used with the long point down. If the point of cut drifts to the short corner (on top at D) the tool will catch, but the leverage is more easily controlled and thus the catches are less traumatic. The acute angle at which the tool lies against the wood also helps. If the tool catches, it's less likely to dig into the surface than when used long point up.

Less experienced turners tend to compound the problem by gripping the tool so firmly that the point of the tool has nowhere to go except deep into the wood. A lighter grip allows the tool to kick back, thereby reducing the damage, though the surface produced is still never pretty.

All the projects in this chapter can be turned using only the skew, but try each with a shallow gouge to see the difference. It's all grist to the learning mill. You can achieve much the same surface using either a skew or gouge, but the gouge is more suited to coves and long curves. You'll find that when cutting detail and decoration the gouge can't get into the corners so easily and that your V-grooves need to be more open. With each tool, the cleanest cut comes when the section of the edge that is cutting is maintained at around 45° to the length of the fibers.

I suggest you start with the long, simple curves and cylinders of the spurtles and rollers, so that you can concentrate on basic tool control and moving with the tool. Or you might prefer the less practical geometric forms such as cones, spheres and

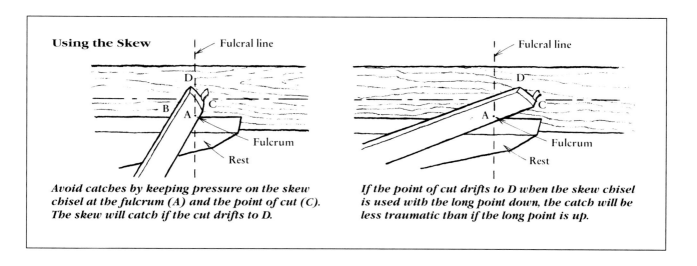

Using the Skew

Avoid catches by keeping pressure on the skew chisel at the fulcrum (A) and the point of cut (C). The skew will catch if the cut drifts to D.

If the point of cut drifts to D when the skew chisel is used with the long point down, the catch will be less traumatic than if the long point is up.

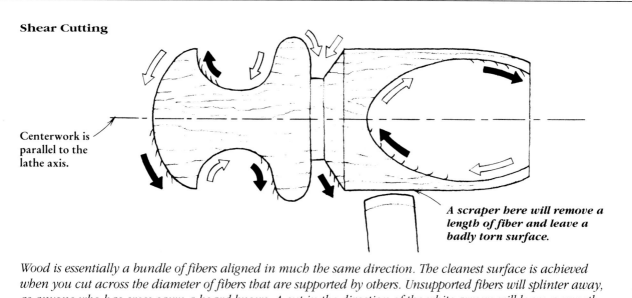

Shear Cutting

Centerwork is parallel to the lathe axis.

A scraper here will remove a length of fiber and leave a badly torn surface.

Wood is essentially a bundle of fibers aligned in much the same direction. The cleanest surface is achieved when you cut across the diameter of fibers that are supported by others. Unsupported fibers will splinter away, as anyone who has cross-sawn a board knows. A cut in the direction of the white arrows will leave a smooth surface; the black arrows will be rough.

cylinders, which are decorative and maintain their appeal if well executed. (I like to use the things I make or that are given to me, so the big checkered sphere on p. 67 has become a doorstop.) Once you are comfortable with the broader forms, move on to the more exacting, repetitious cutting of V-grooves and, finally, beads. Grooves are so much easier to cut than beads that it pays to favor them for decoration at first. I certainly found that beads came a lot easier once I was comfortable cutting grooves with the skew. But there is always a tendency to rush ahead—I did it myself—and to try to cut beads when you've barely managed a V-groove. Try to resist the temptation. If you must cut beads, then go to the section on beads (pp. 54-63).

Roughing Down a Centerwork Blank

Note in the drawing below that scooping cuts are made progressing away from one end to prevent wood from splitting off. If you begin roughing cuts in the center or with the tool

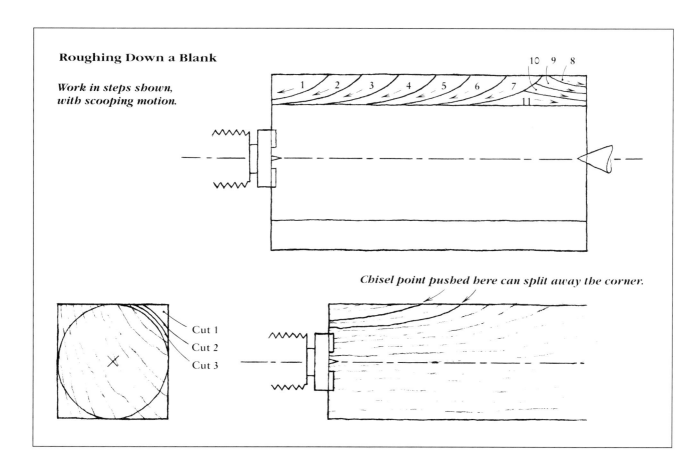

Roughing Down a Blank

Work in steps shown, with scooping motion.

Cut 1
Cut 2
Cut 3

Chisel point pushed here can split away the corner.

Here I use a 1-in. (25mm) skew chisel to rough a 2-in. (50mm) blank from square to round. Being right-handed, I take scooping cuts and work back from the left, as shown in the drawing on the facing page.

rolled into the length of the blank, you risk whole shoulders or corners splitting away, especially when the grain is less than perfectly straight. A chisel point forced into the wood at the arrow could easily cleave along the grain to split away a corner of the blank.

For roughing down, I prefer to use a skew chisel with the long point leading on blanks up to 3 in. (75mm) square, because it saves having another tool on the bench. On blanks less than 2 in. (50mm) square, I'll use a ¾-in. (20mm) chisel. For blanks 2 in. (50mm) to 3 in. (75mm) square, I use a 1-in. (25mm) or 1¼-in. (32mm) long-and-strong chisel. The alternative is a 1-in. to 2-in. (25mm to 50mm) shallow gouge, which I prefer to the deep-fluted versions.

The knocking sound you hear as you turn the square section round changes to a smoother sound as the wood becomes true. If you are roughing down a number of blanks for later use, leave some of the original flatness rather than turning a smooth cylinder, so the blanks will stack nicely on the bench.

Spurtles

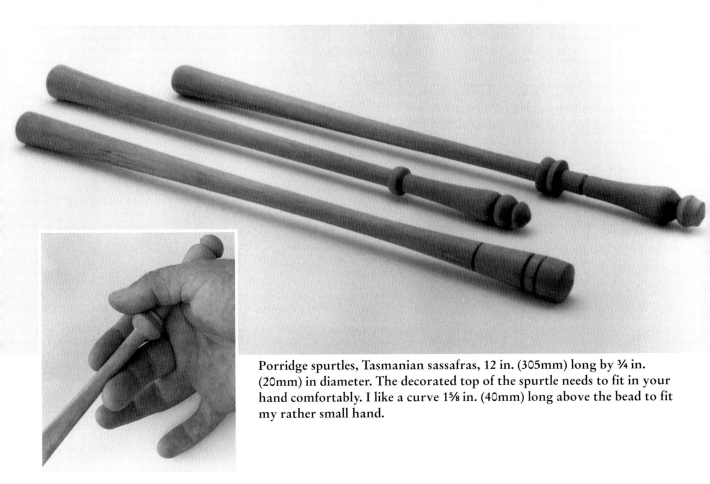

Porridge spurtles, Tasmanian sassafras, 12 in. (305mm) long by ¾ in. (20mm) in diameter. The decorated top of the spurtle needs to fit in your hand comfortably. I like a curve 1⅝ in. (40mm) long above the bead to fit my rather small hand.

S_purtle_ is the old Scottish word for the round stirrer used in making porridge—in Scotland, spurtles still sell widely to tourists as useful souvenirs. The round shape may be a bit limited in use, but carved into a paddle (see p. 16) the spurtle becomes a wonderful spatula, the likes of which cooks cannot have enough of. By using the same principle, you can create all kinds of knives for spreading pâté and butter, modeling clay or for opening letters.

The plain, unadorned spurtle is a simple project that demands little accuracy—as a last resort, you can sand your way to a smooth surface. Conversely, you can make the handle as ornate as you like, but be warned that too many deep grooves become tedious to scrub clean. I like to have a bead to define the base of the handle with a curve above. Establish the overall proportions and curves before refining any detail. Beads look better if they appear to have been applied as an afterthought—the curve should flow beneath. When turning a spurtle, concentrate on overcoming the turner's major vice of pushing, poking and jabbing the tool into the wood and against the axis. Remember that the aim is to make the tool bevel rub lightly against the wood, not to force it against the wood.

Spurtle Handles

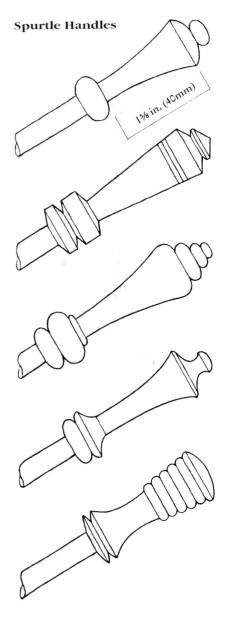

1⅝ in. (40mm)

11

A 3-in. (75mm) diameter length of straight branch should yield four blanks.

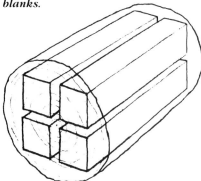

Select a straight-grained blank for this project. Avoid the pith or tight-grained heartwood, since blanks from these are likely to split as the wood dries. The wood need not be seasoned—green wood will work easily, and you can use small branches. Also, as the wood seasons it will go slightly oval, making the spurtle fit the hand more comfortably.

As shown in the following photo sequence, it's usual to mount a spindle between a spur drive and revolving tail center. An alternative is to turn or pare one end of the blank to fit into the hollow drive shaft, as shown in the top photo on p. 45. Lathe speed should be between 1,800 rpm and 2,100 rpm.

Turning a Spurtle

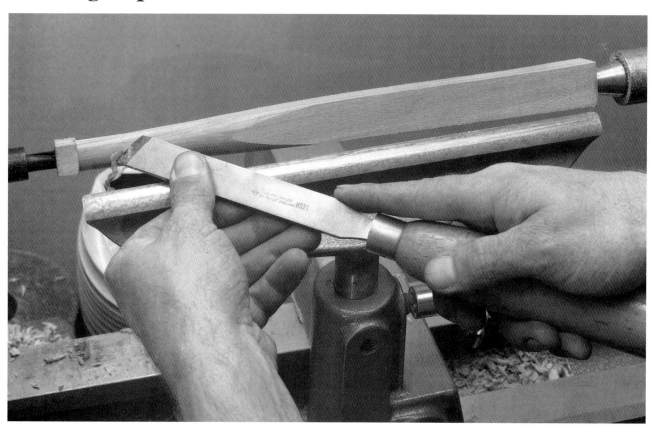

1. Cut a V-groove about a tool's width from the drive to mark the section containing the long point of the center, as well as to provide a neat end to your roughing cuts. As you take roughing cuts and reduce the square to round (see the drawing on p. 8 for the sequence), the wood has less support from the centers; it will flex under the slightest bit of pressure, especially against the axis. You need your hand on the job to keep the wood running true and to equalize any pressure exerted against the wood as you cut.

2. As roughing progresses, wrap your fingers around the length just turned. Your thumb both reinforces the fulcrum and ensures that the tool stays on the rest. If your fingers get too hot, you're using the tool with too much force. Your hand becomes a thermostatic control, warning you of excessive tool pressure against the wood.

3. Once the whole length is round, begin to develop the long curve that will be the spurtle's stirring end. Right-handed turners will find it easiest to cut a long curve working from right to left, using the skew with the long point leading. (Left-handed turners will work from left to right.) As you move the tool to the left—that is, toward your fingers around the wood—also move your left hand, keeping the distance between forefinger and thumb constant.

4. As the spurtle becomes thinner, use your hand as a movable tail-center support—your fingers wrap around the job while your palm keeps the tool on the rest. This grip is safer than it looks. If the tool kicks back, the edge is traveling backward, so it shouldn't cut you; it's more likely that a catch will break the wood. Your other problem at this stage will be the grain picking up in the section where the form begins to thicken for the handle. This indicates that you have begun to cut into the end-grain fibers and that you must cut from the other direction.

5. It's more comfortable to use the skew with the long point up as you work from left to right to turn the handle end. But now the tool lies square to the axis and the wood surface, so you have less control over the line that it cuts. I gain control with an underhand grip, which allows my thumb to ease the tool into the cut while my fingers support the wood. In this situation, the fulcrum has moved to my lower hand, which also keeps the tool pressured against my thumb. If the wood flexes as you cut, you will get chatter marks, which are ridges that spiral around the cylinder. If the surface has ridges in rings, you're not rubbing the bevel on the wood.

6. Above left: A V-groove or two provides simple decoration and softens the otherwise stark form. Be sure to grip the skew firmly, pinning it to the rest so that it can't slide about as you pivot the long point into the wood. The groove nearest the drive will be the parting-off cut, but leave a diameter of at least ½ in. (13mm) to cope with any torque created as you complete the sanding or part off at the other end.

7. Above right: Use the same pivoting cut to begin parting off at the other end, and leave at least ⅛ in. (3mm) for support while you sand.

8. The surface left by the chisel should allow you to start with 120-grit to 150-grit abrasive, but if this doesn't eliminate small ridges, go back to 100 grit or even 80 grit. If you squeeze the paper around the job, you maintain balanced pressure against the axis.

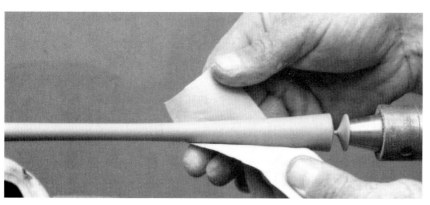

9. If you pull the abrasive against the wood, and therefore the axis, it is easy to apply enough pressure to break the tenuous link to the tail center—hence the need to leave at least ⅛ in. (3mm) of wood in your parting cut. It is better practice to sand before you part in as far as I have here. At this stage, beginners can attempt to part off at the tailstock end, or play it safe and saw away the waste at either end.

Design Variations

Baluster spindles; Simon Raffan, Lilydale, Tasmania, Australia. Note the wood pegs with button tops, which fit the spindles to the stringer.

Rosewood and mahogany cutlery handles; Steve Stafford, Cobargo, New South Wales, Australia. The rigors of use and washing demand that you choose a hard, close-grained wood such as rosewood, yew or one of the fruitwoods.

Turning a billiards cue demands similar grips to control vibration. The brass fittings are installed when the blanks have been roughed with the ends turned true. I mounted each section for final turning with the brass fitting in a jaw chuck to ensure that the job would run true.

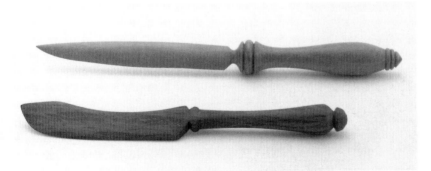

Letter opener (top) and knife for butter or pâté (bottom); Bonnie Klein, Seattle, Wash.

Spatulas

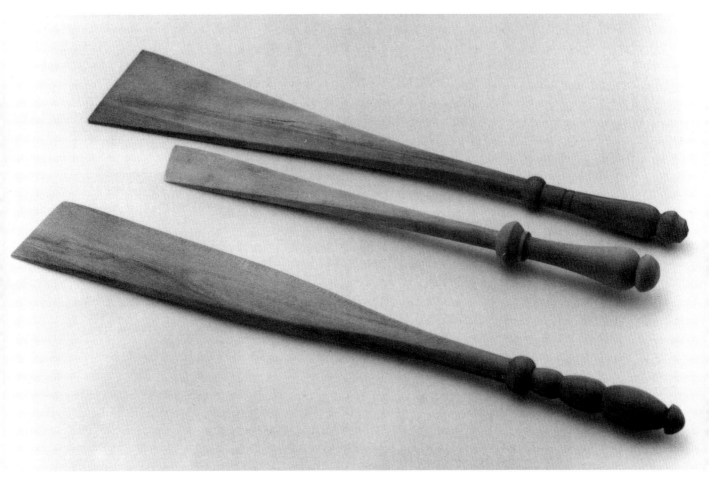

Top and bottom spatulas are 13 in. (330mm) long, with a paddle width of about 2¾ in. (70mm); middle spatula is 11 in. (280mm) long by 1 in. (25mm) wide.

In addition to creating a decorative handle, a variation of the basic spurtle form can involve flattening the stirring section to make a spatula or paddle. The waste can be cut away using a saw, but you need a jig to prevent the blade from grabbing at the rounded form. The belt sander or disc sander is safer and offers more control in shaping. I use a 36-grit belt, which removes material almost as fast as a saw. Lathe speed for turning spatulas should be 1,200 rpm to 2,000 rpm.

Viewed from the side, a tapered blade section adds elegance and makes the spatula nicer to use. Viewed from above, the flared paddles of the upper and lower spatulas in the photo on the facing page are more elegant than the chunky rectangular version in the middle. Flared ends work really well in frying pans, but stirrers need to be narrower and skewed to get into corners easily.

Turning a Spatula

1. For this project, it's most efficient to use a flat wedge-shaped blank, the thickness of which is marginally more than the proposed diameter of the handle.

2. This project gives excellent practice in developing tool control. Here the tool is held in the cutting position, showing that as you turn the paddle section there will be much more space than wood under the cutting edge. If you force the tool against the wood you'll be in trouble, because the tool will enter the gap and act as a lever, breaking the next shoulder of wood as it comes around. To cut a smooth curve, you must manipulate the tool precisely. Otherwise the approach is exactly the same as for cutting a regular blank.

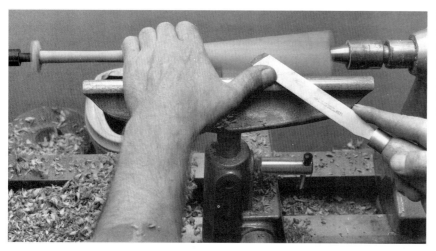

3. Begin by turning the handle end to a cylinder so that you have a smooth, true surface. Use your upper hand to equalize the tool pressure while you cut the paddle section. Decide the line you want to cut, and go for it.

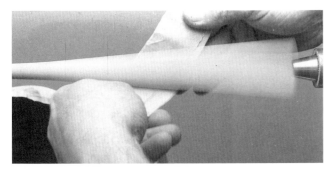

4. To sand the paddle section, stretch the abrasive between your hands and pull it gently against the wood (remove the tool rest before sanding). I never turn the end of a paddle, but prefer to cut it short once the piece is off the lathe.

5. Trim surplus material around the drive-center cone using the skew flat on its side for a peeling cut. Note that my finger and thumb curl around the handle and grip the rest, so that if the job breaks loose at the drive end it won't be damaged against the rest.

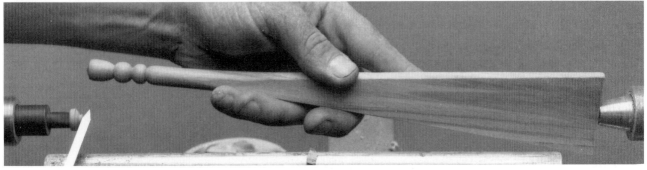

6. For parting off, my hand maintains this position as I pare away material using the long point of the skew. As the final cut is made and the wood ceases to rotate, pivot the spatula away from the rest. Sand and shape the paddle section on the belt sander or disc sander.

Rollers

Rollers, 12⅝ in. (320mm) by
2¾ in. (60mm).

Rollers can be used by cooks, potters or kids (who can always find something to flatten). Small-diameter cylinders can be used as doweling (see p. 24), while larger ones can be sliced and used for inlay, as shown in the photo on p. 123.

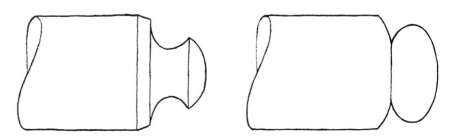

Rollers are exercises in symmetry—the trick is to turn a cylinder with matching ends. Because a cylinder has parallel sides, it is easily measured for accuracy. The ends you turn will depend entirely on your skill level, nerve and sense of adventure, as you risk all. As a novice, I soon learned that it's easy to turn one end with complicated ogees and shoulders, but that to repeat it at the other end is another matter altogether. Unless you have a particularly good eye, I advise keeping your early attempts simple—perhaps limiting decoration to a couple of grooves. Remember that the first end is always easy—it's the mirror image at the other end that causes trouble. My early rolling pins tended to have angular ends and grooves for decoration. If you try beads or rounded ends and have problems, have a look at the section on beads (pp. 54-63) and turn a few dozen for practice.

The roller blank should be about 2½ in. (65mm) square and 10 in. (250mm) long, with the grain running the length of the blank. Keep the lathe speed between 1,500 rpm and 1,800 rpm. At first choose straight grain for easy working, then experiment with twisted grain as your cutting skills develop. Avoid unseasoned wood, which it is likely to split as it dries.

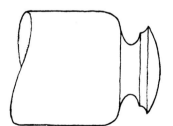
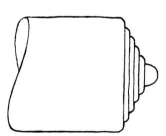
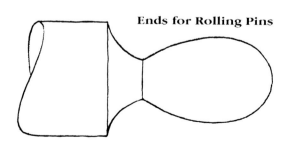

Ends for Rolling Pins

Turning a Roller

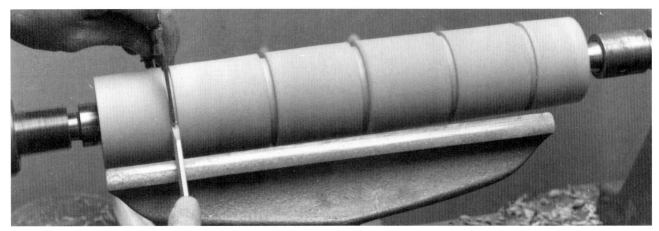

1. When the cylinder is nearly round, use calipers (vernier calipers here) in conjunction with a parting tool to establish the diameter at several points. Use a parting tool ground to a square end or, if you have only a fluted parting tool, use a narrow square-end scraper so that the parting cut has a flat base.

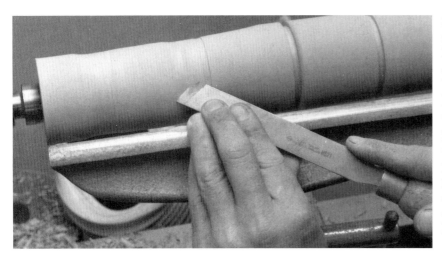

2. To turn the wood to the established diameter, I use a skew chisel with the long point down, and take a shearing cut with the section just behind the point. (Being right-handed, I work back from the left.) Once the waste is gone, take a planing cut the length of the cylinder. By using the tool rest as a jig, you can maintain the cutting point an even distance from the rest as the cut proceeds. The rest profile on this Woodfast lathe is ideal, since I can use the groove as a guide.

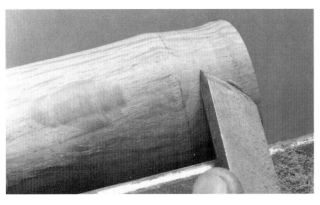

3. To cut the right-hand end, I turn the tool over and work toward the tailstock, because this is easier than bringing the tool in from space to cut a shoulder. It's easier here to work with the long point up; if you work right-handed toward the tail center with the long point down, you force yourself into an uncomfortable and awkward position. I sometimes ease the tool forward to the right using my fingers. An alternative method, shown here, is to use an underhanded grip and push the tool forward with my thumb.

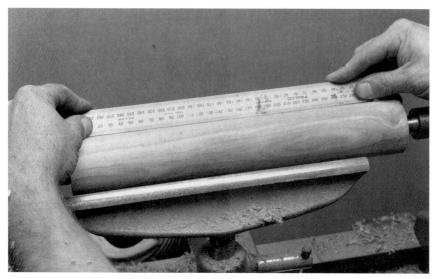

4. Check the surface with a straightedge—the shadow under the edge reveals slight undulations. In this case, a sanding block with fine abrasives will even out small gaps, but larger ones will require heavy sanding or more turning. To mark the high spots, rub the wood with the straightedge to burnish the high spots. If the dips are too big, use calipers to fix a smaller diameter.

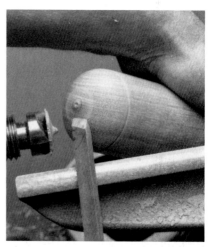

5. Work the right-hand end first so that you retain the maximum amount of material from the drive. Here I opt for a simple conical end with a single decorative groove.

6. When the left (drive) end is turned to complete the sanding, retain at least a ½-in. (13mm) diameter. Any less, as shown in this photo, and you risk the weight and pressure of sanding pulling the fibers from the roller end grain. Saw off the waste ends if you don't want to risk a catch with the skew's long point.

7. With practice, you can part off a roller leaving only a small nubbin for paring and hand sanding.

Turning a Small Roller

1. Dowels are simply small rollers, and turning your own doweling is another exercise that gives a measurable goal. Doweling is useful to have around for plugging holes or the shafts of tops. Approach the task as you would a tiny rolling pin, roughing the square to round, establishing several diameters along the spindle, then working down to a cylinder of that diameter. The jaws of a wrench serve as accurate and durable calipers.

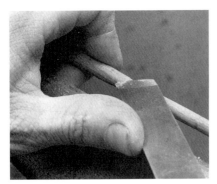

2. Turning doweling is an exercise tailor-made for practicing your range of supporting grips. Here the skew cuts to the left with the long point down, moved forward by my lower hand (unseen). My thumb maintains contact with the rest, offering resistance to the pressure of the tool blade while ensuring bevel contact as the edge eases into the wood. The pressure exerted by my thumb is equalized mainly by my forefinger, while my other fingers curl around the dowel to keep it running true.

3. Cuts made to the right with the long point up require a different set of grips. Here my thumb eases the tool along the rest, ensuring that bevel contact is maintained. My lower hand keeps the tool blade pressured against my thumb so that the cut proceeds under tension. My fingers support the job and maintain contact with the rest (underneath). By extending my forefinger, I gain support and can take a slightly heavier cut. (See also the grips described on pp. 46-47.) And remember: burning fingers equal too much tool pressure.

Design Variations

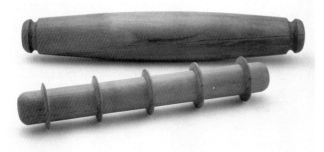

There are several traditional variations for rolling pins, which cater to different culinary needs. A piecrust roller (top) is tapered so that pastry can be rolled thinner in the center. The ribbed roller (bottom) is used for cutting out cookies or making patterns. These make pretty good massage rollers, too, although a row of beads provides the best sensations.

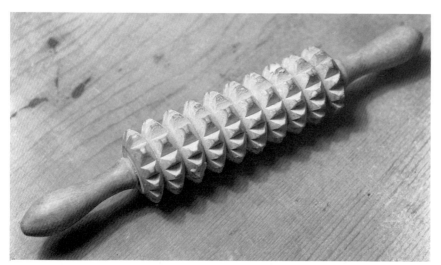

This 8-in. (200mm) pattern roller from a kid's cookery set of 40 years ago has imparted patterns to both pastry and Play-Doh.

Lignum vitae marline spikes for splicing rope; Keith Mosse, Bungendore, New South Wales, Australia. The largest is 17$\frac{5}{16}$ in. long (440mm) by 2 in. (50mm) in diameter.

Dibbles, or dibblers, for gardening. These 10-in. (250mm) garden tools are used for transplanting seedlings and planting bulbs.

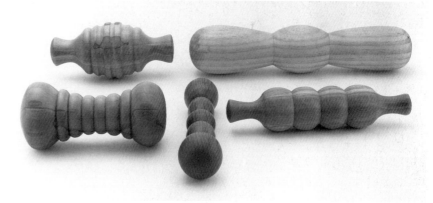

Massage rollers, about 2½ in. (65mm) in diameter. You can create your own exercies in symmetry for specific bodies or parts thereof.

Carver's Mallets

Carver's mallets, 8 in. (200mm) to
10 in. (250mm) long by 3⅛ in.
(80mm) in diameter.

A carver's mallet is is a useful thing to have around your workshop, and it's a good beginner's project. There are few technical demands in the making, but considering several design points will ensure that you enjoy using the mallet you turn. The center mallet shown on the facing page not only looks better than the others, it's also more user friendly. The mallet on the left has too cylindrical a head and too thick a handle, resulting in an unattractive, unbalanced weapon. The other two have better weight distribution, with the heaviest section toward the end of the head and slimmer, lighter handles. Each feels good in the hand, but the rounded end of the mallet on the right means that it won't sit still on the bench, which can be irritating and distracting. By contrast, its neighbor sits solidly on its concave end, ready for action.

The angle between the handle and head should be steep so it won't chafe or blister your hand, and the handle must taper slightly so the mallet won't fly out of your hand as you swing it. The grooves do little to improve the grip, but they do add visual appeal.

Select a hardwood known for its stability and resistance to splitting, such as elm, hickory, *Robinia* or maple. Start with a branch or log 4 in. (100mm) to 6 in. (150mm) in diameter and 10 in. (250mm) long or a similarly sized square blank. In the following photos I use a dry length of Tasmanian horizontal scrub. Don't use absolutely green timber, although the odd split in drying probably won't affect performance. Lathe speed for 6-in. (150mm) diameter blanks should not exceed 1,200 rpm; run 4-in. (100mm) blanks at a maximum of 1,500 rpm.

Turning a Carver's Mallet

1. Here I take the log to a rough mallet shape using a 1-in. (25mm) half-round gouge, although you might find the larger shavings you get off a shallow gouge more fun.

2. Establish the end-grain surface early on so that you know how much wood you have to work with. Allow that the spur-drive cone will penetrate ⅜ in. (10mm). Use a straightedge to ensure that the end is either flat or slightly concave.

3. Rough the handle using the gouge, and enjoy the large shavings.

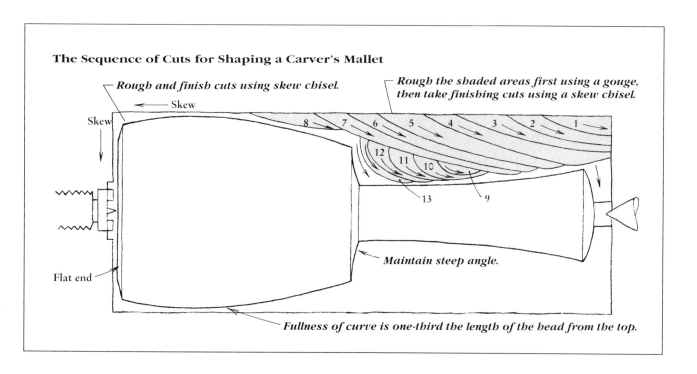

The Sequence of Cuts for Shaping a Carver's Mallet

Rough and finish cuts using skew chisel.

Rough the shaded areas first using a gouge, then take finishing cuts using a skew chisel.

Skew

Skew

8 7 6 5 4 3 2 1

12 11 10

13 9

Flat end

Maintain steep angle.

Fullness of curve is one-third the length of the head from the top.

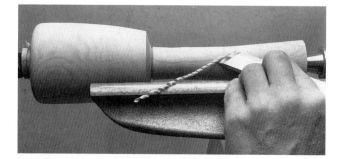

4. Smooth the head with the skew chisel. Keep the fullness of the curve, and therefore the weight, toward the end.

5. Final shaping is executed with a ¾-in. (20mm) skew chisel, its long point leading down the slope. Stop the lathe and move the rest back before testing how the handle feels. To appreciate fully how the mallet will feel in use, take it off the lathe. If you remount it exactly as before, the job will run true. If a remounted job is off-center, it is probably misaligned on the spur drive.

Meat
Mallets

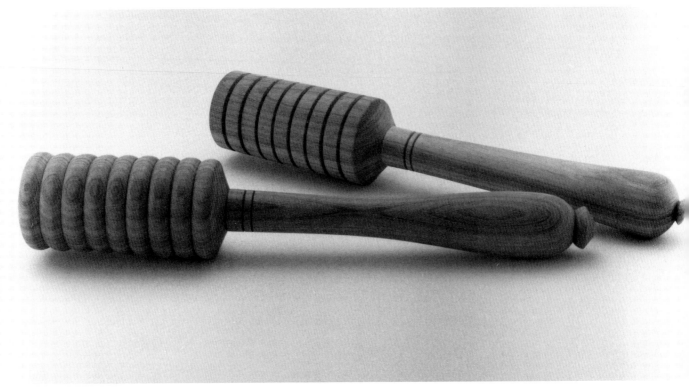

Meat mallets, 13 in. (330mm) long
by 2 in. (50mm) in diameter.

I made my first meat mallets as a production-line item that would provide skew-chisel practice as well as cash flow. I marketed them as meat bashers (which I thought nicely onomatopoeic) for flattening schnitzles, but I soon discovered that people used them on end as pounders or just left them hanging around for decoration.

The basic form is a cylindrical head on a wedge-shaped handle. The head should be about one-third the total length, and although it might look better curved, it wouldn't do the job as well. I turned grooves, coves or beads on the cylinder to provide visual interest while fulfilling consumer expectations that a meat mallet should not be smooth. But more important, I gave myself a tricky exercise in tool control. It is not easy to cut six or more identical coves, let alone grooves or beads, and it is these that provide the challenge.

As a project, the meat basher looks easy. Any competent turner will make a basher in a few minutes, but as a novice you could be occupied for hours with little more than a spurtle to show for the time spent. This is not uncommon, so don't get depressed if you have problems. Just persevere.

The blank should have straight grain and be about 2 in. (50mm) to 2½ in. (65mm) square and 14 in. (355mm) long. Avoid timbers that cleave easily (like cedar, casuarina or oak), because these tend to splinter away in use. If in doubt, see how easy it is to split off a corner with a chisel and mallet. Lathe speed should not exceed 2,000 rpm.

Turning a Meat Mallet

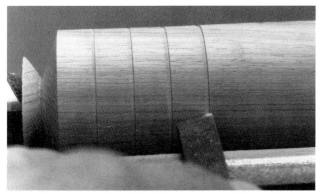

1. After roughing the blank to a smooth cylinder, mark out the grooves or coves that will decorate the head. Locate the head to the left if you're right-handed, so that the long curve of the handle will be easy to turn. I never pick up a ruler if I can avoid it—here I gauge the spacing of the grooves from the width of the chisel. Don't rough out the general form of the basher yet—you'll need to relocate the head to the other end of the blank if you make a complete mess of cutting the grooves. Finish turning the head before working on the handle, allowing yourself maximum room for error.

3. An alternative here is to turn coves. Pin the tool to the rest using a firm grip. Then bring the lower side of the gouge edge through an arc into the wood with the bevel aligned in the direction you want to cut. Start with the tool rolled on its side with the flute facing the center of the cove.

2. Initially cut V-grooves using the long point of the skew chisel with the bevel corner rubbing the wood, but the edge angled clear of the groove side. This is where most novices experience problems, and always for two reasons. The first is that the tool is sliding around on the rest. Your grip needs to pin the tool in a fixed position. Whenever the tool comes into the wood from space, you get maximum control by pivoting the tool on the rest to bring the edge into the wood through an arc, rather than pushing it forward. The second problem is pushing the tool hard into the wood. Again, you need a sharp edge at the right angle, not force, to cut cleanly and quickly. Keep the shoulders between each groove at least ¼ in. (6mm) wide to reduce the possibility of the fibers splitting away.

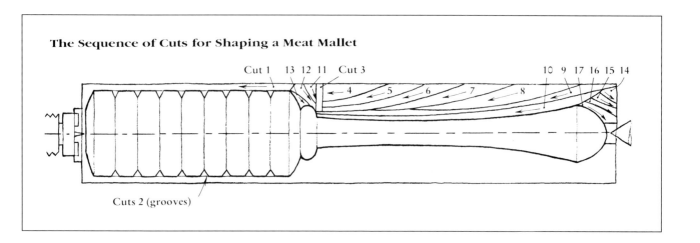

The Sequence of Cuts for Shaping a Meat Mallet

Cut 1 13 12 11 Cut 3   4   5   6   7   8   10 9 17 16 15 14

Cuts 2 (grooves)

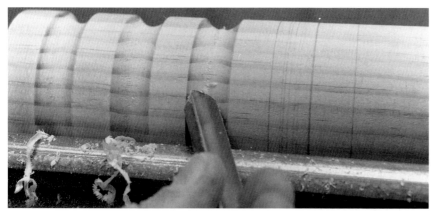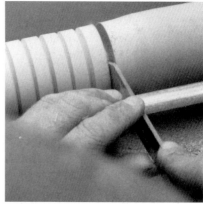

4. Above left: Roll the gouge as you cut into the center of the cove, so that the flute faces up. If the tool catches, you have two options, depending on the type of catch. A nick might require slight widening of the coves, or you can round over the shoulders to create a series of beads. Heavy catches—by which I mean those deep, chipped spirals that are the result of pushing too hard and catching the tool's edge in the bit you've just cut—will require that you cut the cylinder to a smaller diameter. Two or three heavy catches and you soon consider turning your basher into a honey dipper. A few more, and it's on to a spurtle, then spillikans.

5. Above right: Part in at the base of the head, leaving a diameter of about 1¼ in. (30mm).

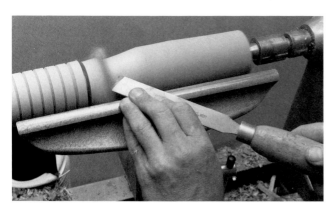

6. I use the skew's long point to shape the handle. Because the tool moves parallel to the axis and I have cut across the grain (with the parting tool), I can take a series of heavy scooping cuts here by pushing the tool toward the drive, breaking away lengths of fibers. As shown in the drawing above, cuts 4, 5 and 11 will split the wood along the grain to the parting cut. It's not very elegant, but it's speedy and effective.

7. As the handle slims, use a shearing cut, easing the point of cut away from the edge to the point of the tool as you come into the corner at the base of the head. You will need to equalize the tool pressure with your fingers to avoid chatter marks. Here I use my thumb to keep the tool on the rest and the bevel in touch with the wood, but an overhanded grip similar to those shown on p. 13 is a good alternative.

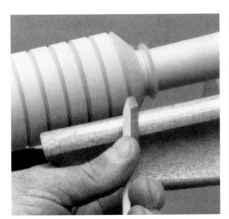

8. Cut the end grain using a shearing cut rather than the skew-chisel point. I find I get the cleanest corner if I make the final cut on the shoulder before cutting along the handle.

9. Take care not to lose the crisp edges of your grooves. Sand the grooves or coves first, then the cylindrical surface. Using a sanding block ensures that you won't round the edges.

Design Variations

Honey dippers, about 7 in. (175mm) long; Simon Raffan, Lilydale, Tasmania, Australia.

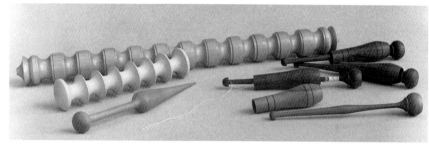

Sewing accessories; Christopher Hall, Mittagong, New South Wales, Australia. At the rear are two thread organizers, at right are German lace bobbins and at left is a tapestry bobbin.

Finials, 4 in. (100mm) in diameter; Nelson Rundle, Auckland, New Zealand. These finials were made to top flagpoles used in the opening ceremony of the 1990 Commonwealth Games in Auckland. Rundle contributed these to dozens of others made by fellow members of the local woodturning society.

Big & Solid

Giant eggs, 7 in. (180mm) to 10 in. (250mm) in diameter.

Turning large pieces is good fun and an opportunity to enjoy quantities of big shavings, especially if the timber is green, although you might need to wear wet-weather gear to protect yourself from the spray of sap. It is difficult to find large dry lumps of timber, so for projects that demand stability, such as bookends, you might need to laminate blanks from dry smaller-section boards. Few timbers are as stable as the grass tree I have used for the bookends on p. 39. Other pieces, such as the eggs on the facing page, can be made from relatively green logs, which are almost certain to split as they season. But this need not spell ruin, because if the defects are sanded or left to weather, the object will soon take on a different character.

Large blanks are usually too heavy for standard small spur drives, which cannot provide a secure enough grip to rotate such a weight. Typically, you switch the lathe on and the wood stays still while the drive mills itself a little hole. It can help to rotate the wood by hand so that it's spinning as you switch on the power, but any load during cutting is likely to have the drive spinning. A better solution is to make up a wide two-spur drive, which can be used on just about any surface and especially on uneven bowl blanks mounted between centers for roughing out.

All the tool-handling techniques used here are similar to those used for smaller jobs, but the lathe runs slower, in this case at 370 rpm.

Turning Big & Solid

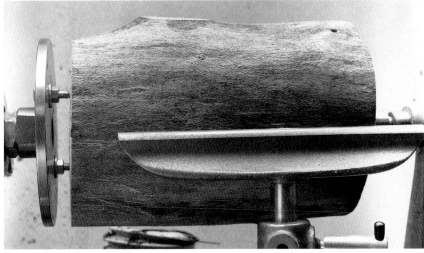

1. I have inserted bolts with sharpened points 4 in. (100mm) apart through a standard faceplate. By punching or drilling ¼-in. (6mm) deep holes in the end grain 4 in. (100mm) apart, I can locate the bolt points securely, as well as ease the task of mounting the heavier blank between centers.

2. I use a 1-in. (25mm) gouge for the roughing cuts, with the handle aligned under my arm and into my side to curb any tendency the tool might have to catch.

3. I take nice fat shavings using a 1-in. (25mm) skew with the long point down as I refine the form of an egg.

4. Turning what will be two sets of bookends, I use the same grips as for smaller-diameter pieces, but have the rest set well above center to bring the tool handle nearer the horizontal, an angle I find comfortable.

5. Here I cut the initial solid into four, creating two flat faces—one for the books, the other for the wall.

Design Variations

Bookends, 10 in. (250mm) high; Anthony Hansen, Goulburn, New South Wales, Australia. The basic form is cut in half along the axis.

Totem poles, 47¼ in. (1,200mm) and 33½ in. (840mm) tall, ranging from 8 in. (200mm) to 10 in. (250mm) in diameter. These have a length of square steel tubing driven into the end grain so that they can be stuck in the ground (and moved around too, unless you plant them in concrete).

Rodents and their spikier cousins, hedgehogs, look good lurking in packs under bushes. These 12-in. (305mm) rodents live under the bamboo just outside my workshop, while others are more difficult to spot. Thinking of thieving the giant eggs perhaps…

Solid vase forms get to look very archaeological with a bit of weathering. Big solid forms are good fun to make between centers and ideal for less-than-perfect material with splits and knots. But avoid material with splits through the heart, because these can easily disintegrate once they're spinning.

Solid Forms for Big Centerwork

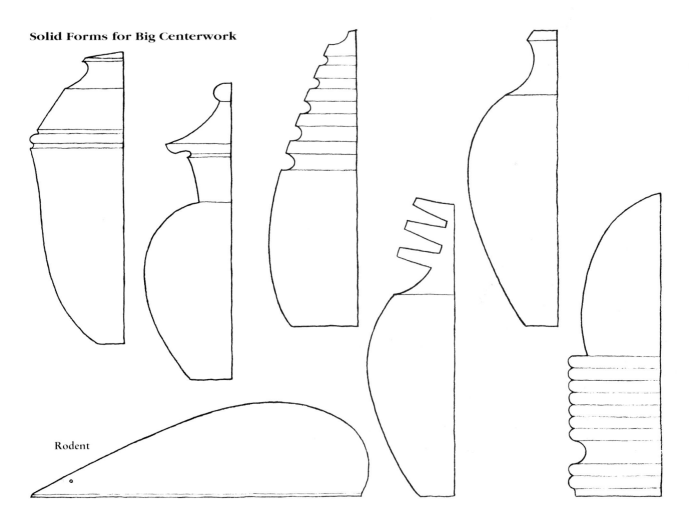

Rodent

Long & Thin

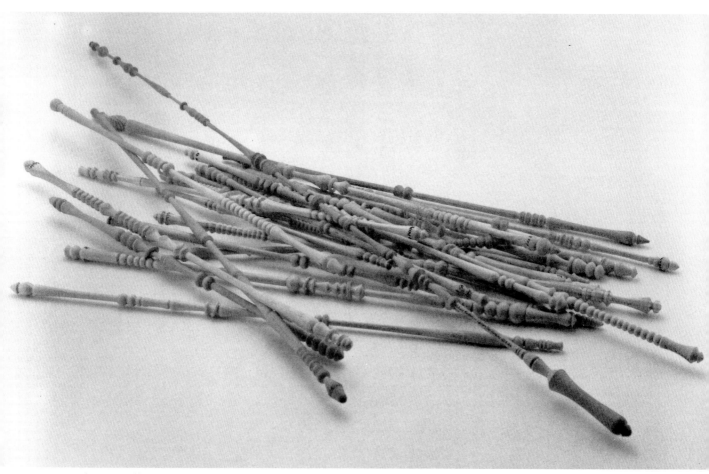

Long, thin spindles, 11 in. (280mm)
to 28½ in. (725mm) long.

A long, thin spindle is widely regarded as one of the most difficult things to turn on a wood lathe. But even inexperienced turners can usually successfully manage a 10-in. (250mm) spindle if they attend to the three problems that commonly bedevil the novice turner—leverage, blunt tools and aggressive tool use. The finished spindle serves no useful purpose other than to remind you that you've been there and done that. But the inner glow of satisfaction once the spindle is complete is well worth the effort and nervous strain, so I call these spindles "ego sticks." Finishing one will give you the confidence to tackle just about any centerwork project.

The spindles in the photo on the facing page were mostly turned as demonstrations in workshops. The longest is 28½ in. (713mm), with the diameters ranging between ⅛ in. (3mm) and ½ in. (13mm). They are unsanded, retaining the surface left by the skew chisel, and all were turned without the use of mechanical steadies or jigs. Long spindles are often supported by a steady, but if the job is as thin as these, the steady can create enough torque to twist the job in two.

The blank for a long, thin spindle must have absolutely straight grain. I prefer radiata pine or pitch pine, which work well and are strong enough to withstand some flexing.

Now to the problems of leverage, blunt tools and aggressive tool use mentioned earlier. To remedy the first, move the rest in as close as you like. To combat the second, sharpen your tools. The skew chisel will need a good edge with little or no burr and a bevel free of facets. A thin spindle is one of the few projects for which I'll use a slip stone in sharpening. That leaves us with that scourge of fine turning: aggressive tool use. Aggressive use of the tools, especially at right angles to the lathe axis, always leads to problems with chatter marks and so on, but here it is catastrophic. Push hard against a long, thin spindle and it will move off-center in the drive and be reluctant to recenter. The secret to turning a slender spindle is to use the same techniques as you did for the earlier exercises in this chapter, but with more finesse—things you could get away with there are disastrous here. You'll need a battery of grips similar to those in earlier projects to support both tool and wood, but now you'll need to use them all the time.

Speed is crucial to limiting chatter. But high speed is not necessarily the answer, because it tends to amplify any whip or flexing; 2,000 rpm is fast enough. If whip is a problem, try a lower speed rather than a higher one.

It is the same with heavier spindles. It is years ago now since I first realized that slow and steady is actually quicker and a great deal less stressful than fast and furious. I was watching the famous English chairmaker Neville Neale turn a 42-in. (1,050mm) long, 1¼-in. (32mm) diameter chair spindle. The lathe ran at about 700 rpm and never stopped. There were no mechanical steadies, and the job took astonishingly few minutes. I knew then that was the kind of skill I wanted. This project will help you on the way, although to get that good takes years.

Turning Long & Thin

1. This blank is about ¾ in. (20mm) square and 16½ in. (420mm) long. Small-section jobs are held easily in the morse taper of the drive spindle, eliminating the bulk of any chuck. Turn or pare the end to fit the taper before driving the blank in with a mallet. If the blank is off center when you bring up the tail center, drive it farther in with a glancing blow to the end to bring it nearer true—it need not be precise, but you must avoid bending the blank. Wind the tail support in tight and start the lathe. Then back off the support until the revolving center barely moves, so that the job is supported but not under pressure.

2. Start to rough out the square to round at the drive end, cutting a V-groove first so the fibers will break away neatly. Use the skew with its long point leading to keep the cuts as near parallel to the axis as possible at all times.

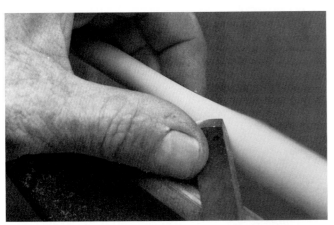
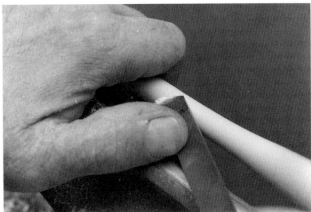

3. As you cut back from the drive you must equalize the tool pressure. Heavier cuts are still possible, but need more support, so I wrap my fingers around the spindle, almost pulling it into the tool edge. My thumb keeps the tool on the rest as well as preventing it from shooting forward into my fingers, in the unlikely event of my pushing hard enough for the tool to shoot forward. If you are left-handed, work back from the tail center.

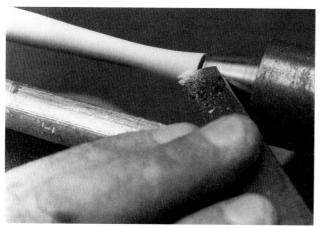

4. Use all the support you can get. Here the skew bevel rides on the tail-center cone as I move the edge into the wood. Once the square is roughed to a cylinder, logic would seem to dictate that work proceed back to the drive from the tail center, to maintain maximum possible strength and mass in the blank and thereby support from the drive. But I find I have a lower breakage rate if I rough out the tail half of the spindle, then turn the detail in the center before returning to finish the roughed end. I find that leaving bulk at the tail support keeps the spindle stiff enough to make the detailing comparatively easy.

5. You have more control turning a bead with the tool long point up, rolling the tool from a flat position onto its side. The thumb moves in behind to prevent kickback, but doesn't push against the tool; the thumb reinforces the rolling action initiated by the lower hand. When the spindle is thin enough to bend, the tendency for the rotating wood to climb the cutting edge increases, and controlling this becomes the main problem. If you don't, the blank tends to shift in the chuck and you end up with a crank-shaft effect. In these and the next few photos, note that to keep the spindle running true I use my fingers to keep pressure on all sides.

6. Remove waste to the base of the bead with the skew's long point leading. Use the edge to make a shearing cut and minimize torque, rather than the point, which would pry the fibers to a frill and obscure your vision.

7. You have to use the point of the tool into the corner, and curls are to be expected if you are working farther into the wood than the base of the bead. Take a small pivotal cut with the long point of the skew to continue the curve of the bead across the fibers. If you go a fraction too far, the minuscule line you'll leave at the base of the bead will detail the corner. When you turn the center beads before the tail-center half of the spindle, you gain rigidity, but you must use even less pressure to avoid the torque that can twist the fibers apart, or breakages where there is twisted or cross grain.

8. I make cuts into the base of the bead from the left with the long point up, because of the difficulty of handling the tool the other way up in my right hand. I don't care to chance the spindle to the less secure technique of my left hand. The tool is eased along the rest and into the cut by my thumb; the tool hinges on the end of the handle. Note how my fingers in each grip reach down the spindle to provide more stability, working as a sort of movable tail center.

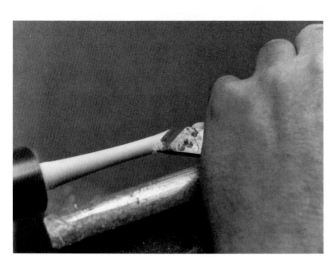

9. As soon as possible—when the spindle is nearly cylindrical—I start to cut toward the drive, even if it means cutting slightly uphill and into end grain. This compromise cut allows me to take a comparatively heavy shaving, because all the energy is absorbed straight into the drive. Sand before you begin to part off at the drive. Don't pinch or wrap the abrasive around the spindle, because it won't take much in the way of stress. Don't apply wax while the job is spinning on the lathe, because the stickiness of the wax tends to grab the polishing cloth.

10. Because the job is held in the drive shaft, you can support the spindle with your left hand, back the tail center off, then turn the end. This always impresses onlookers in a demonstration, but it's not as difficult as it looks if you can stand the heat. I move the spindle off center, then pull it back on to the chisel to take a fine shearing cut across the end grain. Think in terms of moving the wood rather than the tool, even though you'll need to ease the edge slightly to the right as you cut.

11. When parting off the spindle, brace your forearm on the rest over the tool blade to prevent lateral tool movement, while pivoting the long point into the wood.

12. The completed spindle is 15¾ in. (400mm) long and ⅛ in. (3mm) in diameter at its midsection, with loose mini-rings. I leave my ego sticks with the finish left by the tool, and date each one so that I can ponder my progress (or otherwise) from time to time.

Design Variations

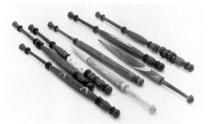

Lace bobbins; Malcolm Fielding, Silverdale, Lancashire, England. Fielding uses a range of fine hardwoods, bone, mother-of-pearl, brass, titanium and other man-made materials to create his superlative collection, of which this is a tiny sample. These bobbins are 4⁵⁄₁₆ in. (110mm) long by ³⁄₁₆ in. (5mm) in diameter.

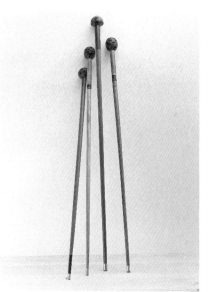

Walking sticks; Don Lee, Mogo, New South Wales, Australia. The upper sections of these canes were predrilled to accept a steel rod through the center for strength.

Rocking chair; Neville Neale, Rugby, England.

Spillikans or pick-up sticks. Make the box first. It's much easier to turn sticks to fit a box than a box to fit sticks. These days I fit 35 7½-in. (190mm) long sticks into a box made from a 2-in. square blank, with an internal diameter of 1⅝ in. (40mm). Go for a slightly larger box with an internal diameter nearer 2 in. (50mm) in case your sticks aren't quite as thin as you imagine; if they are, you can always make more. The sticks are little more than fancy dowels. If there is a bead in the center of the design, I move the bead slightly on each stick so they all fit into a smaller box than would be needed if all the beads were in the same place. (I learned that one the hard way).

Loose Rings

Baby rattle, 1⅝ in. (40mm) in diameter by 4⁵⁄₁₆ in. (110mm) long.

A solid ring of wood on a goblet stem or, in this case, a baby rattle, is a bit of woodturner's trumpery that rarely fails to intrigue the uninitiated, who tend to think that the ring has somehow been forced onto the spindle. In general, avoid wood that splits easily for this project, because if the short grain in the ring is inherently weak it won't stand knocks. Lathe speed should be about 2,000 rpm.

Turning a Loose Ring

1. Rough out the ring as a deep, straight-sided bead. The tighter the fit of the ring, the greater the dramatic effect.

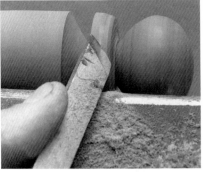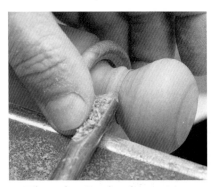

2. Above left: Begin by rounding over the top of the bead.

3. Above right: Use the skew's long point to undercut the bead from either side to develop the ring. A long bevel on the skew allows you to approach from a more acute angle, making it easier to round the underside. When the ring is almost severed, you'll hear the brittle sound of thin wood. Sand the ring before you separate it—you'll probably need to start with 80 grit to round the underside facets.

4. When the ring has been separated, hold it to one side as you turn the shaft. The tight curve and working space demand the use of a small shallow gouge. In this situation, my lower hand (unseen) keeps the tool blade pressured against my thumb, setting up the tension between the two hands, which allows me fine control of the edge.

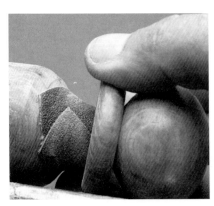

5. When the spindle is turned, create a small drum sander by wrapping abrasive around the spindle as shown (remove the tool rest when sanding). I use old self-adhesive sanding discs, but you can rely on friction to hold the abrasive in place, or something sticky like double-sided tape. If you hold the ring and switch on the lathe, you can sand the inner parts as well as the outer by waggling the ring. Working through the abrasive grades is tedious, so the cleaner you cut the surface, the better.

2. Cutting End Grain

The problem of how to cut end grain cleanly without the fibers tearing out besets practitioners of every woodworking activity. Most woodworkers deal with end grain by hiding it away. But this is impossible for turners unless the job is a plain cylindrical spindle, such as a chair component, where each end is hidden in a mortise. The moment a spindle is adorned, be it with a shallow cove, V-groove or bead, the end grain will be exposed to a greater or lesser degree. It is therefore essential that turners learn to shear-cut the wood fibers.

In this chapter, the blanks for all the projects are gripped at one end only, with the grain aligned parallel to the lathe axis. This is still centerwork. Blanks must generally be turned between centers to fit the chuck you use. Don't forget to retain a bit of the flat face from the original square so that the blanks stack easily before use. You'll be able to turn several pieces from one blank, but don't be overambitious. The farther you work from the chuck, the more leverage you'll have to contend with, so keep blanks 6 in. (150mm) long or less.

Beads

Jewelry beads, ½ in. (13mm) in diameter, turned for a jewler and ready for finishing.

The best way to learn tool control is by cutting beads and small grooves using a skew chisel. The skills, which exemplify the art of hand turning, are learned only through constant repetition, as you strive to make one bead identical to another.

The key to cutting beads lies in maintaining tight control of the fulcrum by having the pressure of one hand resist the other, so that the tool can be pivoted and rotated precisely in a series of arcs. The catches that occur when you fail to do this are usually aggravated by excessive tool pressure against the wood and the axis.

If you cut beads on a spindle between centers, you'll waste wood. By contrast, individually turned beads can be used as components for jewelry, wheels for toys, frivolous decoration or just displayed in a bowl. Or what about a bead curtain?

The size bead you make will depend on its intended use. For jewelry, a ⅜-in. (10mm) to ½-in. (13mm) diameter is ideal, and will present fewer problems than other sizes, even though the process is the same regardless of scale. Lathe speed should be around 2,000 rpm. Usually you can get several beads from one blank, and if you turn a true cylinder using the methods described on pp. 22-24, the beads should be the same diameter. The probability is that each bead will be slightly different, but once you've turned several dozen you should be able to match up pairs. This is the way sets of hand-turned knobs or chess pieces are matched—hundreds are turned to the same pattern, then sets are created where minute differences are hardly noticed.

Turning a Bead

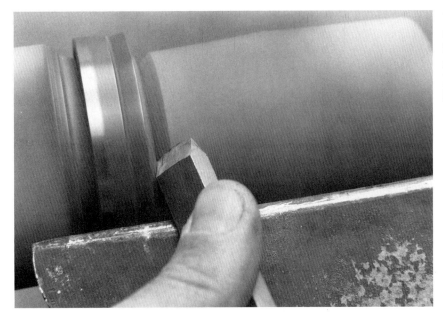

1. Whenever you mount or remount a blank in the chuck, you must true it up so that you know exactly how much wood you have to play with. It's also a good opportunity to see how the wood works.

3. Then cut to the right and true the rest of the blank.

2. After you cut a small V-groove, work back from that point in a series of scooping cuts. The fibers will terminate tidily at the V-groove, rather than building up in a fan.

4. Don't forget to true the end grain. This is always a good time to take several fine shearing cuts, just for practice. If you have a catch, it won't matter too much, and you'll gain the confidence needed to tackle similar cuts when hours of work are at risk.

5. Small blanks can be mounted straight into the drive spindle rather than a chuck, but make sure that your lathe has a hollow drive shaft, which will allow you to knock out the waste with a rod.

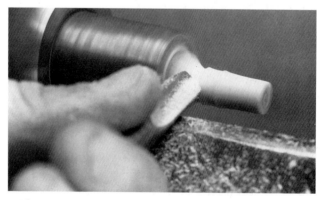

6. If you are turning expensive or rare tropical hardwoods or bone, as shown here, use cyanoacrylate glue to attach short sections to an expendable waste block, using the tail center to align the blank.

7. In these photos, I make a ball that is 1¾ in. (45mm) in diameter with a hole through the center. Any drilling should be done before the bead is turned—there's no point in turning the bead and then risking its ruination by drilling off center. If you drill a straight hole first, then have a catch, you end up with a smaller bead, maybe two. To begin, use the skew's long point to make a small conical recess at the center of the blank, which will help line up the drill. Keep the tool flat on the rest, like a scraper. The technique is the same whether you are drilling into end grain or cross grain.

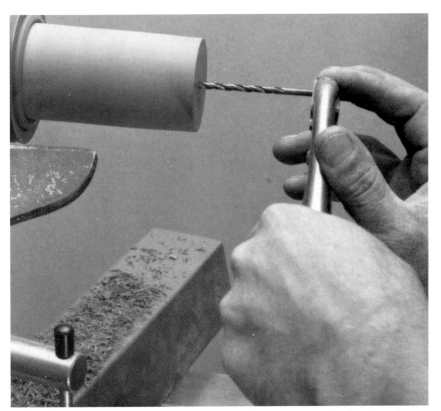

8. I usually hold small drills in multigrip pliers. Present the drill bevel to the left side of the cone just as you would a gouge bevel, then align the drill with the axis and push. A sharp drill will go in easily if aligned with the axis. Partially withdraw the drill every ½ in. or so to clear out the compressed waste that builds up in the drill flutes (be careful—it gets hot enough to burn your fingers).

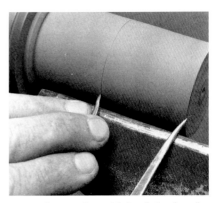

9. Mark out the width of the bead, measuring from a flat end-grain face. Check this with a straightedge, such as your skew chisel. This is to be a sphere, so set the dividers to the diameter of the cylinder. For real speed, you can turn a cylinder whose diameter equals the width of your skew, then use the tool to measure the bead width, much as when laying out the grooves on the meat basher (see p. 32).

10. Use a parting tool to define the width of the bead, cutting to the headstock side of the line at right angles to the axis and in about one-third of the diameter.

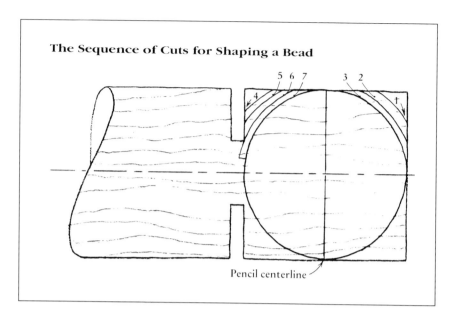

The Sequence of Cuts for Shaping a Bead

5 6 7   3 2

4   1

Pencil centerline

11. Mark in pencil the center of the roughed bead, then use the skew chisel to develop the curve. Begin the cut with the long point up and the bevel riding on the pencil line. Then pull the tool onto the rest with your upper hand, ensuring that it moves neither sideways nor forward on the rest. This is a grip that sets up tension—the forefinger pulls the tool to the rest, the thumb resists pressure exerted by the fingers on the other side of the tool, and both resist any movement initiated by the lower hand.

12. Use your lower hand to rotate the tool to the right until the edge begins to take a shaving. When you see a fine dust rising from the edge, pivot the tool on the rest and sweep the edge through an arc or series of arcs, repositioning the upper hand as required. Use caution when making cuts 2 and 3 so you don't roll the tool too far into the wood and lose the spherical curve. When the tool is rolled over to near vertical, take the tool away, turn it over and continue to cut the curve using the long point. Use a similar grip for cuts 4 to 7, but roll the tool to the left.

13. The result should be a cleanly cut, nearly polished surface. Any minute facets and burnish marks will sand away easily enough, leaving a smooth surface ready for finishing, which is done before parting off.

14. Part off using the skew's long point. Make sure your catching hand doesn't grip the bead and spin it off the wood remaining in the chuck—this will tear the end grain and spoil the finished ball. Hand-sand any slightly torn end grain around a drill hole. With a bit of practice, you'll find that you won't need the centerline to gauge the curve, and that your proficiency at shearing minimizes or eliminates sanding. After turning, arrange beads in a groove so they can't roll about. Small ones are sorted most readily with tweezers. And remember that often your pairs will be separated, as happens with drawer knobs or earrings, so that they never have to suffer close comparison.

Plugs and Chucks

Often at the end of an end-grain project you will be left with a stub protruding from the chuck. Always keep these. You can create a stock of small disposable chucks or you can turn thin disks to use as inlay, as shown in the lower right photo on p. 123.

True the stub to a cylinder. If you want plugs for drilled holes, use a template, as shown on p.164.

Part off a disc.

It pays to roll the parting tool to the left when the disc is almost free. This makes a small V-groove that allows you to lever the disc free with a little handle, which will be enormously useful when you come to test-fit the plug as an insert.

Design Variations

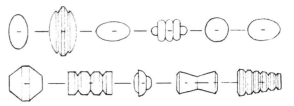

A Selection of Bead Forms for Practice

To get practice, you'll need to make groups of small identical items. If you create a form you like, try to repeat it — it's the discipline of repetition that really hones turning technique. You need to know what you're trying to make and to have something to aim for. The drawing shows a few forms to go on with.

Necklace of African blackwood and silver; Ray Norman, Australia. The beads are a maximum of ½ in. (13mm) in diameter. I chose African blackwood for its weight — the heavier such beads are, the better, so tropical hardwood offcuts proved ideal.

These fine Swiss chess pieces made in the early 1960s vary slightly from one another. Such minute differences occur no matter how skilled the maker, and lend character to the overall set. A copy-lathe version of the same pattern would look dead by comparison; any greater variation would look inept.

Eggs; Anthony Hansen, Goulburn, New South Wales, Australia. Eggs are one of the most difficult objects to turn, if the result is to be smooth of curve and looking as though it was laid without some unfortunate bird suffering severe internal injuries. Few hand-turned eggs are as fine as these, which are devoid of any bumps or painful pointy ends.

Door latch; Simon Raffan,
Lilydale, Tasmania, Australia.

Massage tool; Bob Thomas,
Canberra, Australia. The ball-like
wheels are 1¾ in. (44mm) in
diameter, and the handle is 8 in.
(200mm) long.

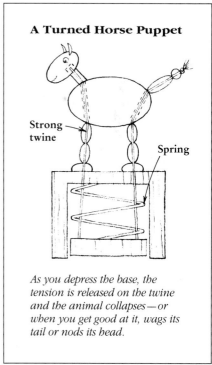

A Turned Horse Puppet

Strong
twine

Spring

*As you depress the base, the
tension is released on the twine
and the animal collapses—or
when you get good at it, wags its
tail or nods its head.*

Clown (left); Eric Horne, Topsham, England. The toy measures 3 in. (75mm) in diameter at the waist. The horse
puppet (right) is the product of East German mass production. It is made up of various beads held together with
two lengths of strong twine; one piece controls the head and front legs, and the other works the tail and hind
legs. The parts are threaded starting and finishing at the top, with the tail knot frizzed and the head knot
covered by the head as it's glued onto the neck.

Large Spheres

Spheres, 4 in. (100mm), 4½ in. (115mm) and 5¼ in. (135mm) in diameter.

While I'm sure these wouldn't qualify as spheres in engineering terms, micrometers being so persnickety, they still manage to roll around enough to require containment in a dish. Spherical forms are always pleasing and consequently quite decorative enough to have rolling around the house. They're good fun to make, being much the same as a bead, only on a larger scale. Lathe speed should not exceed 350 rpm.

Turning a Large Sphere

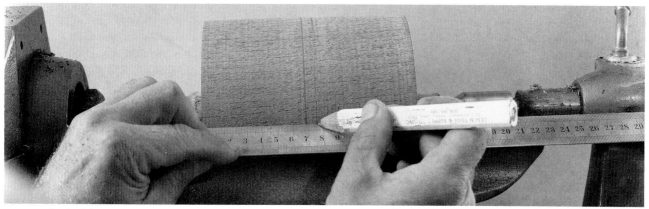

1. Rough the blank to a cylinder and part away the ends until you have a square-ended cylinder where the diameter and height are equal. Then mark the center. I measure slightly over halfway from either end. The center is midway between these two lines. I switch on the lathe and shade in the space between. From now until you sand, the shaded area should stay pretty well intact.

3. I part in as far as possible, then saw off the waste in case I pull out the end grain in the form.

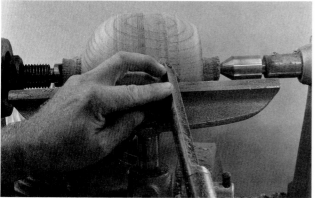

2. I use a 1-in. (25mm) half-round gouge to remove the corners. Take care not to curve the form too tightly away from the pencil shading.

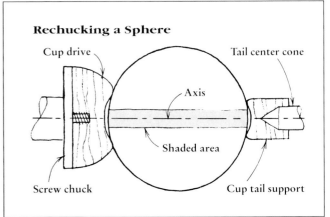

Rechucking a Sphere

Cup drive

Tail center cone

Axis

Shaded area

Screw chuck

Cup tail support

4. The form is now rechucked between cup centers, with the center of the shaded circumference aligned to the axis. The centers are both turned from scrap material. The drive is mounted on a screw chuck and easily made. The tail support has to be made to fit over your center cone. If you have a drill the same size, drill a hole in the blank and mount the blank on a mandrel to turn the cup end.

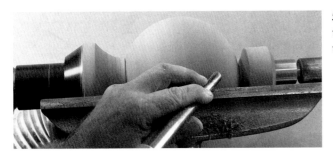

5. I use a ½-in. (13mm) shallow gouge to turn away all the surplus material, which can be seen on the top of the form as you turn.

6. Stop and check your progress when the form is nearly smooth. You should still be able to see the line you marked around the circumference, which is now a slight ring around the form. In this case, I overcut on the other side of the sphere, because I failed to align the shaded line accurately with the axis, so I must rotate the blank between the centers.

7. With the blank realigned, you can see the lump that needs to be turned off the top section of the shaded area.

8. I use the same shallow gouge to scrape-cut the surface to a smooth sphere ready for sanding. A small portion of the original shaded surface remains to be sanded away. If the form is still ovoid at this stage, mark another circumference, as shown in the top photo on p. 65, and go through the process again to create a smaller sphere.

9. I pad the centers with soft cloth to limit bruising and burnishing during sanding. Realign the sphere frequently to ensure even sanding of the whole surface.

Design Variations

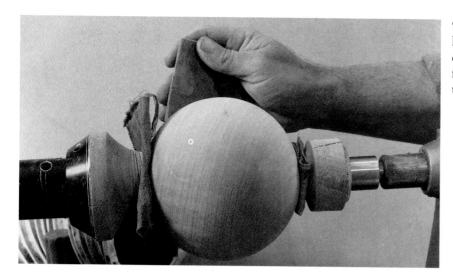

Laminated sphere, 10¼ in. (260mm) in diameter; John Hill, Burrawang, New South Wales, Australia. Small sphere and cone; Richard Raffan.

Spinning Tops

Tops, 1⅝ in. (40mm) in diameter.

Tops continue to fascinate long after childhood; in some parts of the world, young men can even gain favor in ritual courtships by winning top-spinning competitions. The one-piece tops shown here are more suited to teenagers and adults, who can snap their fingers, than to small children, who generally can't. They provide a most frustrating exercise for the inexperienced turner, but are excellent for developing a delicate touch. And you don't waste much when things go wrong…which they tend to do at first.

The aim is to cut a cone with a nice sharp point on top of a little shank. The shank needs to be slender for a good spin, because these tops are snapped into action between finger and thumb. Weight is crucial for two reasons. First, too heavy a top is difficult for most people to spin well. But more important, because the tops are made with the shaft toward the headstock, the heavier the cone is in relation to the shaft, the more difficult they are to turn, because, as you soon discover, a thin shaft can't lend much support to a heavy cone. The simple solution would appear to be to turn the shaft first, so that the cone points to the headstock, but if you do that you can't turn a really sharp, dead-center point. And if the point is off-center, the top will oscillate rather than spin true.

The angle of the cone point needs to be 90° or less. A flatter cone demands an upright spin (with the shank vertical), which is not so easy, whereas this becomes less critical with a sharper point. Both the appearance and feel of the shaft are improved if it's slightly curved—a cylindrical shaft is pretty boring.

The best spinners are between 1 in. (25mm) and 1⅝ in. (40mm) in diameter with a shank diameter of ⅛ in. (3mm). For the blank, choose seasoned wood of even grain and density. Dense hardwoods like cocobolo or ebony always look good and spin well. Work with 4-in. (100mm) lengths initially, to keep chatter to a minimum, and set the lathe speed for 2,200 rpm. When you turn the blank true, ensure that the end grain is cut cleanly, with no fibers pulled from the center. If this is a problem, you are trying to cut too quickly. The pace of the cut has to slow as you near the center, because the wood is

Turned Tops

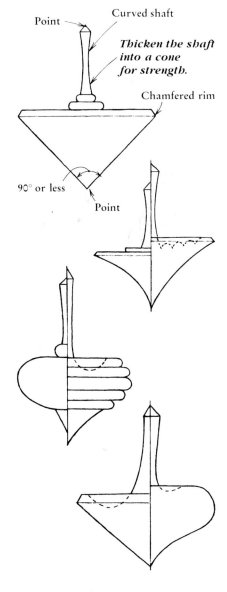

Point

Curved shaft

Thicken the shaft into a cone for strength.

Chamfered rim

90° or less

Point

moving faster than the rim. Learn to stop the tool at the center. It doesn't matter if you push the tool edge across the center on a convex surface, but on flat or concave end grain you are likely to have a catch. This applies to all gouges and chisels on both face and center work. The rate at which you ease the tool into the timber must always slow as the diameter decreases. Practice the habit as you work through this section.

Turning a Spinning Top

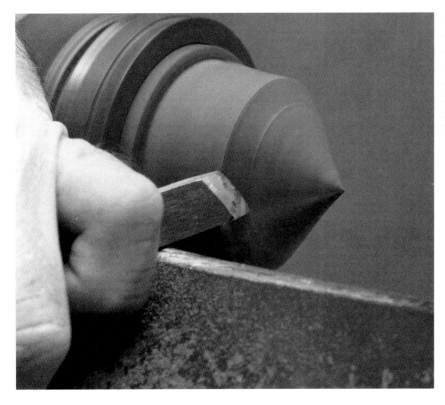

1. Use the skew with its long point down so you can see what you're doing. I use the point of the tool for roughing, but a shearing cut for developing the point of the top. Proceed very gently and steadily into the center, so that the point will barely need sanding.

2. Aim for a near-polished surface off the tool. The slight burnish mark from the tool bevel near the rim will sand out with 220-grit abrasive.

3. Begin to cut the back of the cone, but don't proceed too far until you have completed the rim. I suggest chamfering it slightly. Definitely avoid sharp rims, which will not only chip, but can cut you, either as you turn or later. Turning the back of the cone is the most difficult part of this project—embark upon it only when the cone and rim are as good as you can get them, because later rectification of a poor cut will be exceedingly difficult. Stop the lathe and check carefully before you proceed, something I find most students fail to do with amazing consistency.

4. As you open the groove to create space to work on the back face of the cone, you reduce the support running through from the chuck. The thinner the shank becomes, the more you need your upper hand to equalize the pressure of ever lighter cuts. Any tool pressure against the wood will leave chatter marks. Continue to use the long point of the skew. Deepen the groove to leave around one-third the diameter of the cone, then take a light final cut in from the rim on the back of the cone.

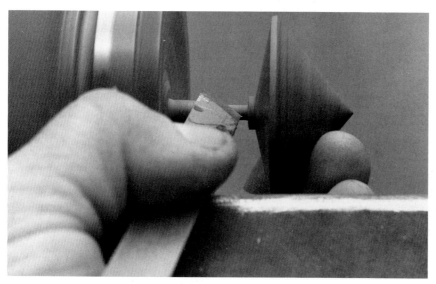

5. Once the back face has been cut, try not to touch it again with the tool. Leaving a small, flat bead saves further cutting on the end grain, while adding some strength to the junction of shaft and cone. Other solutions are suggested in the drawing on p. 69. For a curved back face, use a small, shallow ¼-in. (10mm) gouge. You should be able to cut cleanly enough that a light touch of 220-grit sandpaper will finish the job. Heavy sanding is out of the question because the thin shank won't take the stress.

6. To part off, take a shearing cut with the long point leading. By pushing the tool forward firmly, the top should drop into your hand with a reasonable point. If you sand the end of the shank round, you'll have a top that can be spun either way up, as you can see on p. 68.

Design Variations

Pull top, 3 in. (75mm); Eric Horne, Topsham, England. Horne painted the back of the cone to enliven an otherwise bland piece of beech.

Two-inch (50mm) diameter pull top; Anthony Hansen, Goulburn, New South Wales, Australia.

Bottle stoppers, turned to 1⅝ in. (40mm) in diameter. Cork sleeves are available from woodturner's supply stores. As shown in the drawing below, the size of the shank will depend on the diameter of the hole in the cork sleeve.

Bottle Stoppers

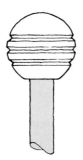
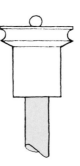

3. Hollowing End Grain

The difficulties of working end grain increase once you start to hollow into it. Because you can't generally move the rest any closer than the rim of the object's opening, the further you cut into the wood, the more leverage you must contend with. To control leverage in the confined working space, you must use longer handles on heavier-section tools. In addition to this problem, you often can't see what you're doing, so you have to work by feel.

And then there is the problem of shear cutting the fibers. Any portion of the internal form that tapers from the rim toward the depth of the hollow should, in theory, be cut from the center back to the rim. To achieve this at speed, trade turners traditionally employed a technique called back-hollowing. Using a shallow gouge with the flute facing the axis and cutting from and on the far side of center at about 2 o'clock, the bulk could be cleared out in seconds. The gouge is almost upside down, cutting the fibers as they travel upward. Back-hollowing developed out of necessity, because most old lathes in production shops had long rests fixed for turning spindles—the rests couldn't be moved at right angles to the axis. The technique enabled speedy hollowing of thick-walled, low-cost treen, such as egg cups or boxes, where scant consideration was given to the precise internal form provided it was cut cleanly. Although the cut is clean, I never regarded its slightly ridged surface as smooth or precise enough, so I complete the shaping using a scraper. The more common approach today is slower, with cuts made into the center from the rim. You attack the work the same way you might approach a large bowl with the grain across the face. This means that the cut butts into the end grain and that the surface is always slightly rough, but this too can be easily smoothed with a scraper.

When working on projects where the end grain is to be hollowed, it pays to complete the inside before turning the exterior form. The thin walls are extremely weak and easily split or shattered by any pressure away from the center, either during cutting or sanding. External pressure is not as much of a problem, since it tends to compress the form, though vibration will split a thin wall soon enough. You need the strength of the whole blank for support as you hollow into end grain, as well as a pretty good idea of the overall form as you start, in contrast to facework, where you hollow after establishing the overall form.

The classic production solution is to allow plenty of wall thickness as a hedge against variations and problems, a chunky-but-safe approach to design that continues to blight the craft today, spawning a vast array of heavy wooden trivia on the gift market. Little of this arouses awareness that the lathe can be used to create objects of infinitely more aesthetic appeal. With a little effort and more attention to detail on the part of turners, this situation could be changed. Better designed objects don't take any longer to produce than badly designed ones, but they will sell faster, and offer better value for the money.

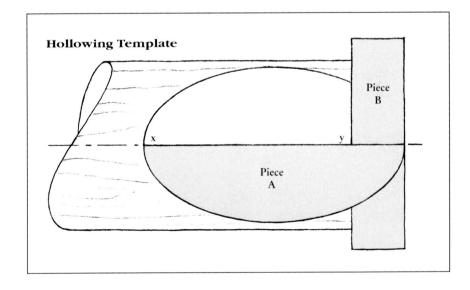

Hollowing Template

Piece B

x   y

Piece A

Where accuracy or consistency is required, you can gauge the internal space with a template, which you can make of ⅛-in. Masonite, wood or plastic (see the drawing on the facing page). On piece A, cut the half-profile of the space to be hollowed out, with side xy representing the centerline. Piece B is a rectangle of no particular dimension, but longer than the diameter of the project's opening. Attach piece A at 90° to piece B, so that the distance xy equals the intended depth of the internal space.

To use the template, stop the lathe, and place piece A inside the hollow, with piece B resting against the rim of the project's opening. Continue hollowing until side xy aligns with the center when piece B has double contact with the rim.

Little Bowls

Small bowls, 2³⁄₁₆ in. (55mm) in diameter.

I have made thousands of these little bowls as marketing props for my small scoops. They are about as good an introduction to hollowing end grain as you can get, especially if you want to master the back-hollowing technique. Failures don't waste much material, and there is the design aspect as well. The difference between good, adequate and bad bowl forms on this scale is very fine, but you have the opportunity to experiment without the capital outlay required for larger pieces. The aim is a simple bowl of sound form. The inside should belly out slightly from the rim—aesthetically, this creates a shadow, which displays the form, but it is also practical in a small utilitarian bowl used on the table for salt, sugar or spices.

I don't normally recommend making bowls with end grain across the base, because the grain structure is so weak that a heavy knock can push a hole through it, and, with larger forms especially, radial splits are probable if there is any tight heartwood from around the pith. But you should have few problems with these little bowls if you make the bases about ⅛ in. (3mm) thick.

In production work, I make five bowls from one 8-in. (200mm) long blank that is 2 in. (50mm) in diameter, but the leverage while turning the outer two bowls is such that novices should start with 4-in. (100mm) lengths up to 2½ in. in (65mm) diameter. Lathe speed should be in the 1,750-rpm to 2,100-rpm range. Once you have trued the blank, bring the rest across the end grain for hollowing.

Cut a few bowls in half to check the wall profile. The outside curve of the bowl on the right would look better if it swept in to a narrower foot, and the top of the internal curve should be fuller where it undercuts the rim, but the thickness of the base is ideal at about ⅛ in. The bowl on the left has better curves, but the walls are too thick.

Turning a Little Bowl

2. Alternatively, you can set the rest at the same height as for hollowing in from the rim, but start the cut up into the face before arcing back to center. Keep the flute rolled toward the center to avoid catching the left shoulder of the edge.

1. For back-hollowing, use a shallow long-and-strong gouge ground with a long bevel and full-curve fingernail edge. Set the rest height so that the point of the horizontal gouge is at center. The shearing cut is made from the center on the far side of the axis, between 2 and 3 o'clock.

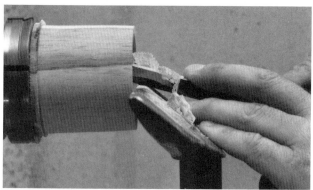

3. When the bowl is roughly hollowed to a depth of ⅞ in. (22mm), refine and smooth the curve using a round-nose scraper. Set the rest so that the blade tilts up a few degrees when the tip is at the center. The scraper should be ground with a long left curve and be as large as will fit the hollow. I always select a scraper whose edge curves only slightly tighter than the curve I want, rather than trying to sweep a narrow, tight-curved edge accurately through space. The weight of the larger tool also helps dampen any tendency to catch. Start the smoothing cut at the rim with the tool angled upward for a shearing scrape, cutting only to the fullness of the form, or you'll butt into end grain. As the cut proceeds, you'll need to raise the handle a bit to reduce the leverage.

4. For the second stage of the scraping cut—smoothing the ridges—begin at the center. By dropping the handle as the cut proceeds, you angle the edge toward a cleaner shearing scrape and develop a smooth curve as the edge moves through an arc. In general, smooth movement of the edge, either backward or forward, in the horizontal plane will lead to smooth curves. The act of raising or lowering the handle takes the edge through an arc in the vertical plane. If you can do this while easing the tool forward at a constant rate, the edge will travel in a spiraling parabola, cutting a parabolic curve with greater ease than if the tool is kept horizontal. Sand the inside before working on the outside to create a finished surface to work to. If you sand both surfaces at once, wall thickness will be difficult to assess, and heat build-up from the abrasives may split the wood.

6. If you chamfer the base and add a groove for decoration, you have a good, serviceable little bowl or egg cup, which needs only to be parted off, then reverse-chucked for the base to be finished.

5. Mark the exact inside depth on the outside of the bowl and part in on the drive side of the line, as shown in cut 1 in the drawing on p. 88. Here you see two ways of pinching the parting tool firmly to the rest. The advantage of having my fingers on top is that I can deflect the shavings, although I don't get such a clear view of the cut as it progresses. It's tempting to provide for potential disaster by putting the depth mark nearer the chuck, but this is a bad idea—you'll inevitably lose track of the point you're working to and end up with too thick a base.

7. Here is a more traditional bowl form ready for sanding, showing the surface typically left by the skew.

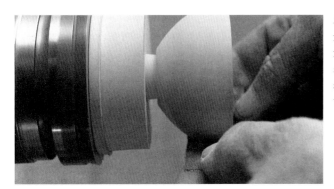

8. To maintain a crisp edge to the rim, sand the sides first and then the rim, rather than rolling the abrasive from one surface to another. Beware of heavy sanding against the axis. It's easy to pull the bowl off the small spigot of short grain, leaving you with a ragged hole in the base of your bowl.

9. Once the bowl is parted off, the base needs finishing. It can be flattened on a sander, but will look better if it is turned. You can turn a taper on which to reverse-chuck the bowl from the stub still in the chuck, although if you are making several bowls, it's better to save them up so you can do one directly after another and develop a rhythm. Don't forget to save stubs like this for chucks or inserts. Turn the shallow (1° or 2°) taper using the skew chisel as a scraper flat on the rest. Make sure that the bowl rim fits the chuck shoulder—this will align the bowl and help keep it running true. If the bowl fits snugly but slips slightly, dampen the taper with water or use a layer of tissue paper.

10. My hand braces the bowl, ensuring that it won't fly if it comes loose. I keep the tool blade pressed against my thumb as I pivot the point across the end grain to dish the base slightly.

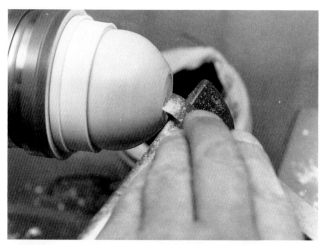

11. If the bowl is fixed securely to the chuck, decorate the base with tiny grooves using the long point of the skew, or scrape with the short corner to turn a recessed base. Or do both, as shown here.

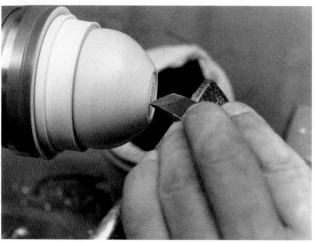

Scoops

Scoops, 4 in. (100mm) long by 2 in.
(50mm) in diameter

I have made around 45,000 scoops, and I reckon that in the 1970s they paid all the basic bills while doing wonders for my turning technique. My design was based on a vague memory of a Georgian silver sugar scuttle, although the final product hardly reflects this.

The scoop is conceived as a stem beneath an elongated bowl or cup, which is partially cut away to create the scoop. It is essential to appreciate that the bowl bellies out from the rim and that the curved wall is of near even thickness. The thickness of the wall can vary slightly without compromising the form if both the inside and outside are smooth curves. But, as many plagiarists have shown, a cumbersome look is the reward if you get it wrong. Scoops are not as easy to make as their form might imply at first glance, let alone at the speed required to be competitive.

These scoops have to be turned, not drilled. Anybody can drill a hole into end grain and chop the end off at an angle, but I regard scoops made this way as ugly in their angularity. What we are after here is a form altogether more sensual.

This very early, well-worn scoop of mine has shoveled demerara sugar for 20 years. Today I find the handle embarrassingly chunky and the bowl too heavy and steep shouldered. The two might have been turned separately and then joined.

Avoid fresh-felled wood for scoops—the bowl can distort off-center and the handle can split as the wood dries. The grain should be fairly straight, but this is not as essential as it is for a thin spindle. The curves mean that you cut mostly across the grain and can cope with the odd twist, especially in the bowl. Start with a blank 2 in. (50mm) to 2½ in. (65mm) in diameter, 4½ in. (115mm) to 5½ in. (140mm) long. Larger or smaller blanks create problems, so are best avoided initially. Run the lathe at around 1,800 rpm.

Scoop Forms

The three upper scoops fail for various reasons, both visual and practical.

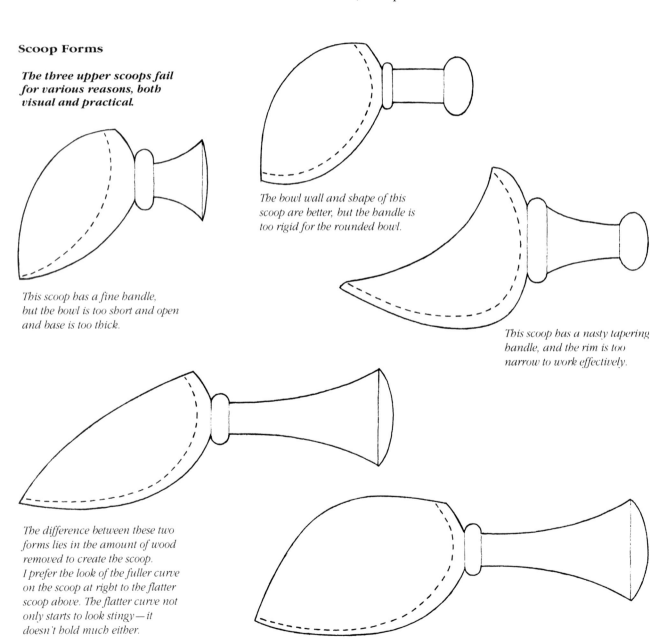

The bowl wall and shape of this scoop are better, but the handle is too rigid for the rounded bowl.

This scoop has a fine handle, but the bowl is too short and open and base is too thick.

This scoop has a nasty tapering handle, and the rim is too narrow to work effectively.

The difference between these two forms lies in the amount of wood removed to create the scoop. I prefer the look of the fuller curve on the scoop at right to the flatter scoop above. The flatter curve not only starts to look stingy—it doesn't hold much either.

Turning a Scoop

1. After truing the blank, I back-hollow into the end grain using a ½-in. (13mm) half-round gouge, which removes the bulk in a few seconds. As with the little bowls, I always finish the inside before shaping the outside to maintain the maximum amount of supporting wood; if you turn the outside shape first, you make the task of hollowing infinitely more difficult. If you are turning only one or two scoops, you might find it helpful to drill a depth hole before starting to hollow. In addition to indicating the correct depth, the hole makes the back-hollowing cut easier to start.

2. With the bulk removed, use as wide a scraper as possible to complete the hollowing. The tool should have a long left curve, which flows from the side of the tool, eliminating any corners that might score the surface you've just cut. Develop the fullness of the internal curve by undercutting the rim, and think in terms of reaching into the far corner of the hollow from whichever direction you are working. Make sure that the internal bowl depth is at least equal to the outside diameter.

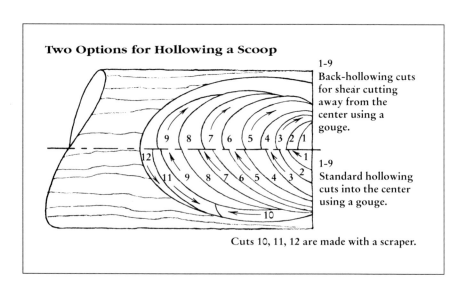

Two Options for Hollowing a Scoop

1-9
Back-hollowing cuts for shear cutting away from the center using a gouge.

1-9
Standard hollowing cuts into the center using a gouge.

Cuts 10, 11, 12 are made with a scraper.

3. Mark the exact internal depth on the outside of the blank. If you put the mark nearer toward the headstock to allow for error, you'll lose track of exact depth, which makes turning an even wall more difficult and time-consuming. Sand the inside before beginning to shape the outside. This way you'll remove any pencil marks and establish the surface to which the outside relates. There's a safety issue too: If you sand the inside and outside together, it is easy to develop a sharp rim that can cut you to the bone like a bacon slicer.

4. Develop the curve into the rim using a skew chisel (shown as cut 2 in the drawing below). If you feel comfortable with the skew and are cutting with minimal pressure against the axis, you will find it more efficient to make the parting cut first (cut 1), then turn the whole bowl. It's a simple matter of time and motion: you pick up the skew one time less.

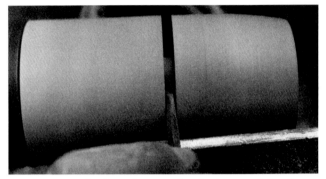

5. Part in on the line that marks the internal depth. Obviously, if you cut too far you will have a curious sort of napkin ring, but listen and you will hear danger approaching as the cutting sound changes pitch. You can learn the finer limits here only by parting a few bowls off and remembering the sound at severance time. In general, part in to just under half the original diameter.

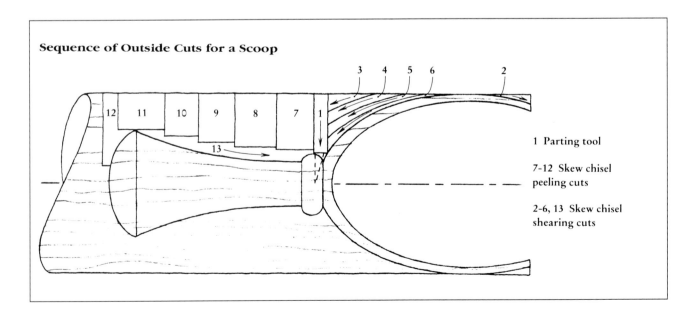

Sequence of Outside Cuts for a Scoop

1 Parting tool

7-12 Skew chisel peeling cuts

2-6, 13 Skew chisel shearing cuts

6. Cut the curve using the skew chisel. Initial cuts with the long point can be heavy, provided the force used is parallel to the axis, because the fibers that split along the grain will break free at the parting cut. The idea is to project, in your mind's eye, the curve you're cutting to the point where the headstock side of your parting cut would intersect the axis.

7. Continually check wall thickness. Your fingers will become reliable calipers, though it's safest to check mechanically to confirm that you have what you feel you have. Never use calipers to measure wall thickness while the lathe is running. An alternative, but slow way to ensure consistent wall thickness is to drill a hole or two in the portion that will later be cut away. Then all you have to do is stop the lathe and peer through. This also eliminates the possibility of scoring the interior with the calipers.

8. Develop the handle. You can use a gouge, but it's faster and more satisfying to step it out with the skew chisel flat on the rest for a peeling cut. Use a square-section skew for stability, rather than an oval-section one, which will wobble about.

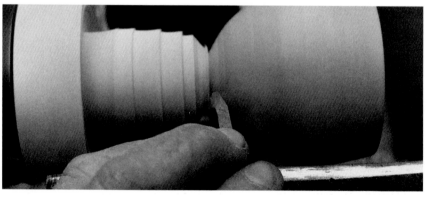

9. Refine the base of the bowl with the skew's long point.

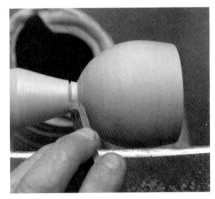

10. Take a cut from the end of the handle to the base of the bowl to establish overall proportions.

11. Use the skew's long point to develop the bead and refine the handle. Put a curve on the handle—straight lines are harsh and not nice to fondle.

12. Take a shearing cut with the long point leading to shape the end of the handle.

13. Now sand the outside. Any pressure directly against the axis must be equalized by your fingers on the opposite side if you are to avoid pulling the piece free. I never apply an oil finish at this stage because it collects dust when I sand the saw cut later. If you use a hard finish, such as varnish or sealer, there should be no problem.

14. Part off using the skew's long point. Your hand prevents the scoop from hitting the rest as it comes free.

15. Turn a taper chuck upon which to mount the scoop so that you can turn the end. Make sure that the rim abuts the chuck shoulder for stability. This is a tricky operation, and in production I find it faster and less nerve-racking to sand the handle ends smooth on the belt sander.

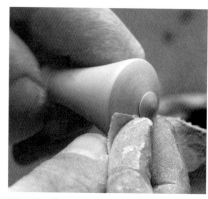

17. You'll need plenty of support to keep the scoop on the chuck as you sand the end, because the pressure of the abrasive tends to pull the job off-center.

16. Here I use my hand to support the scoop as I turn the end. My thumb acts as a fulcrum for the tool as well as a pad between scoop and rest should the scoop come loose. Because the fixing is tenuous, use the point of the skew rather than taking a shearing cut, so the wood won't roll up the tool edge, which is its natural inclination.

18. I use a bandsaw and grip the scoop's handle firmly to prevent the piece from rolling into the blade at the start of the cut. My fingers are behind the blade so that if it does snatch or shatter, my fingers are clear of the teeth. (Alternatively you can sand away the waste. Remove the bulk on a 40-grit to 60-grit belt sander or disc sander, then finish with 120 grit to 180 grit.) Once the blade has entered the wood, problems should be over, because the back of the blade supports the form. Pull the scoop through the blade, pivoting it slightly to develop the curve. Always err on the side of caution—bits cut off can't be replaced, while undercutting is easily sanded away.

19. Sand the curve smooth. This is easier on a belt sander than a disc sander because all parts of the abrasive move at the same speed. Keep the curve fuller rather than flatter. To speed production, I make three standard scoops from blanks ⅞ in. (22mm), 2 in. (50mm) and 3 in. (75mm) in diameter, using runs of one wood so that I don't have to adjust to different sounds and densities for each scoop. Speed dictates that I make only one scoop from the large and small blanks, but two from the mid-size one. The small ⅞-in. (22mm) blank is 2½ in. (65mm) long. This is knocked straight into the drive-shaft morse taper. I turn two 2-in. (50mm) diameter scoops from blanks 8 in. (200mm) long. The square blanks are roughed between centers. The 3-in. (75mm) diameter blanks are 6½ in. (160mm) long.

Design Variations

Baby rattle. The wall needs to be slightly thicker than for a scoop—around ¼ in. (6mm) thick.

Massage ball, probably Chinese. The ball is turned from very dry material, the holder from a green limb. The ball is forced through a hole just large enough to take it. As it dries, the holder shrinks around the ball.

Antique set of egg cups. I particularly like the way the turner used the screw hole in the base to locate the cups on the stand—not much wasted effort there.

Miniature beef bone goblets; Michael Dixon, North Ireland. These tiny turned pieces are less than ½ in. (13mm) tall.

Miniature scoops or goblets can be turned from a small piece of beef bone glued with cyanoacrylate super glue to a waste block in the drive spindle .

Turning proceeds as usual with standard small tools such as the ¼-in. (6mm) gouge and ½-in. (13mm) skew chisel.

Internal shaping requires special little scrapers, which you can easily make from concrete nails or the tang of an old tool.

Plant Forms

Plant forms, 2 in. (50mm) in diameter.

Plant forms can serve as the basis for a whole range of spindles to fill your weed pots and vases, or you can mount them in clusters on a log. Run the lathe at 2,000 rpm.

Turning a Plant Form

1. Use a chuck for the drive and tail-center support, and a length of branch for the blank. First true the center portion of the blank. Note how I swivel the gouge to obtain the biggest shaving, keeping the cutting portion of the edge at about 45° to the wood. Green timber is ideal. It's easier to work initially, and as it dries it distorts to create a less contrived form. This blank is 8¼ in. (210mm) long.

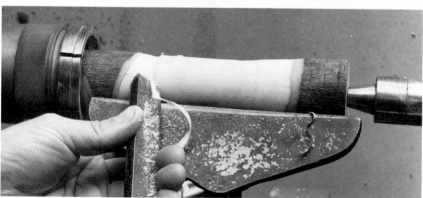

2. First, hollow the inside using either a gouge or skew. With a bark or eccentric rim, it is easier to cut a smooth curve working in from the rim, whether or not you use the tail center.

3. I use a ½-in. (13mm) shallow gouge to cut away the waste below the head.

4. I take a shearing cut to smooth the underside of the head. Note how I pivot the long point of the tool into the wood, then drop the point further and take take a shearing cut just behind the point.

5. When the head is turned, you need to back off the tail center and finish the inside of the head. Use the long point of the skew or a small gauge to remove the cone of waste, then sand the head. I use a folded cloth to protect the wood and lend enough support to keep the head running true while I turn the stem.

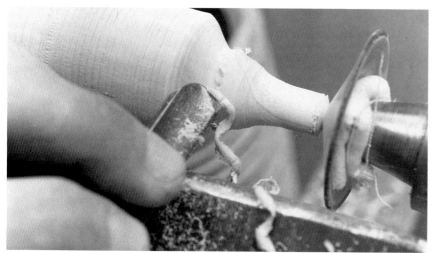

6. The stem is turned and sanded in stages to avoid the stress that would be placed on the slender spindle if the sanding were left until the turning was completed. I turn away the bulk using a ½-in. (13mm) shallow gouge, taking particular care not to exert pressure against the axis.

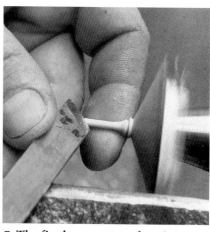

7. The final cuts are made using a ½-in. (13mm) skew.

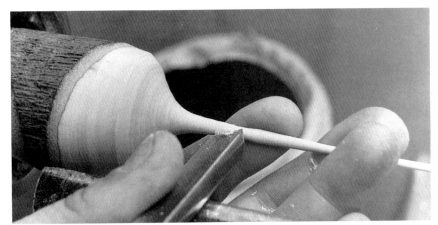

8. This 7-in. (180mm) long stem was completed in four stages using all the support techniques practiced in turning the long, thin spindle (see pp. 45-48). I try to avoid making straight stems; a long shallow curve is more interesting.

9. To decorate the end, I use the point of a ¼-in. (6mm) gouge because there is not enough room for the skew to operate.

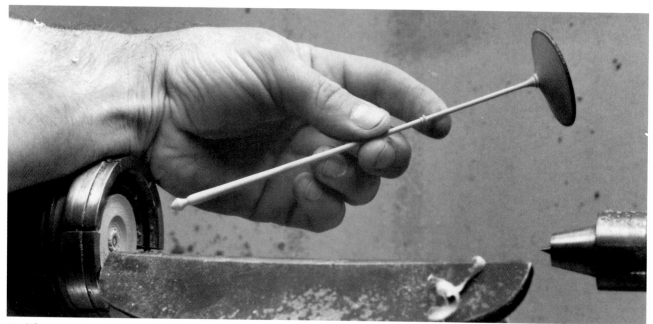

10. The completed form is parted off using the skew's long point.

Design Variation

"Forest flowers"; Anthony Hansen, Goulburn, New South Wales, Australia. The tallest of these forms is 8 in. (200mm).

Tall Vases

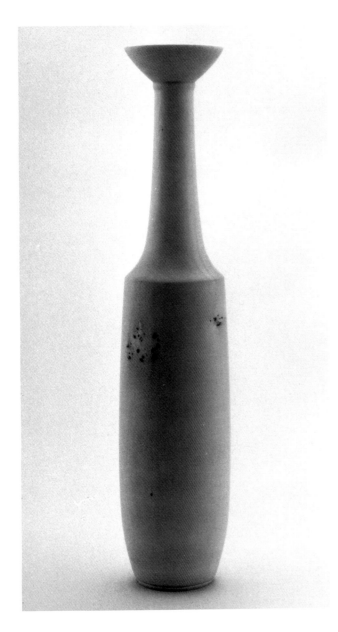

Vase turned from Huon pine, 15⅜ in. (390mm) tall by 3⅛ in. (80mm) in diameter.

Vases are popular wherever a society or culture supports purely decorative possessions. For a vase is essentially a decorative object, even though it is practical enough to contain flowers. A wooden vase is suited more to arrangements of dried plants, although the inside can be sealed to hold water as effectively as ceramic, metal or plastic.

As a decorative object, a vase can usually find a home, filling some alcove or creating a focal point on a table. If the curves and proportions are strong enough aesthetically, a vase can stand on its own, though vases this good are rare. But while searching for truly satisfying forms, you can also enjoy the other challenges that making a tall vase presents.

A vase would be easy if it were solid and turned between centers (like the forms shown on p. 41), but it's not. Instead, it needs to be held in a chuck so the end can be hollowed. The blank is first held between centers while the form is roughed, the foot turned to fit the chuck and the base finished. The job is then remounted, gripped only by the foot; this can mean hollowing into end grain 15 in. (380mm) or more from the chuck, where the slightest catch or pressure against the axis will lever the blank from the chuck. The solution is to use a steady, which supports the job in place of the tail center for the hollowing and internal sanding, after which time the job can be mounted between centers for completion. Lathe speed should be 1,500 rpm to 2,000 rpm.

Turning a Tall Vase

1. Begin by roughing the form of the vase between centers. I turn and finish the base to fit my chuck (here a collet chuck), leaving the conical recess from the tail-center cone as a design feature. Because the form swells from the foot, I need to cut a groove for the chuck jaws to grip. The groove also looks good as a decorative feature, so the uninitiated are unlikely to realize its true purpose. Remember to sand and finish the base and foot, which will be in the chuck now — you don't always get another chance — and about 1 in. (25mm) above the groove that will be faired into the rest of the curve as the outside is completed.

2. I remount the job, using about four layers of cotton cloth to prevent the metal of the collet jaws from staining or bruising the rim of the foot. I adjust the steady — a standard accessory for this Woodfast lathe — so that the three wheels bear on the neck of the vase. You can use the tail center to ensure that the job runs true, but with practice and a good eye, you can get the job to run true without it. Just rotate the lathe by hand and pull the end in as required.

3. Hollowing proceeds as for a scoop or small bowl, although the steady allows you to use quite heavy cuts to remove the end grain. Just as with the scoop, I make the inside first. But since the wall profile won't be revealed, unlike a scoop bowl, I don't need to take quite the care with the internal form.

4. To extend the hollow, I use an auger to drill a center hole to within 1 in. (25mm) of the base. An elastic band around the shaft acts as a depth gauge.

5. To sand the inside, I use self-adhesive abrasives wrapped around a dowel. You can use 60-grit abrasive to fair the turned and drilled sections into a flowing line.

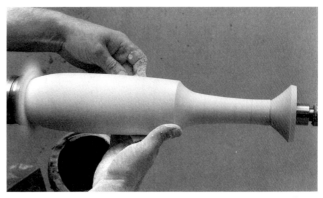

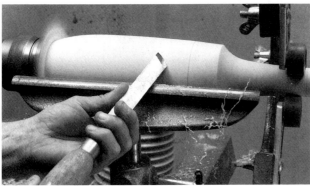

7. For sanding, I remove the steady and bring up the tail support, being careful to support the end rather than pressure it, which might split the neck. As shown in the drawing below, I use a plug in the neck if required. Attach a rescue cord to the plug or wrap it in cloth to make sure you can get it out easily. Don't push the abrasive against the surface or you'll split the neck.

6. Move the steady to allow work on different sections of the vase, but ensure that the surface for the wheels runs true. You might find it tempting, once the inside and top are sanded, to bring up the tail center and finish the job between centers. But with the grain running the length of the vase, the fibers can easily split with any pressure from the tail center wedging into the neck or a little catch exerting pressure against the axis.

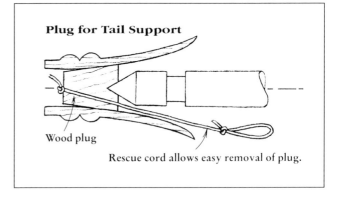

Plug for Tail Support

Wood plug

Rescue cord allows easy removal of plug.

8. A few days after completing the vase, I remounted it between centers for modification. By slimming the neck and making the underside of the rim convex rather than concave, I lightened the form.

Design Variations

Smaller, lighter-weight vases—often called weed pots—can be made between centers if the blank is predrilled off the lathe. This enables you to mount the blank over a drive mandrel equal in diameter to the size of the hole, while the tail center supports the other end. The mandrel can be a short length of dowel held in a jaw chuck. Wet the end of a dowel so it expands for a better grip. Alternatively, turn down a short length driven into the drive spindle, as shown on p. 57.

These barrel spigots can be made by drilling the hole so that the blank fits over a mandrel.

Pepper Mills

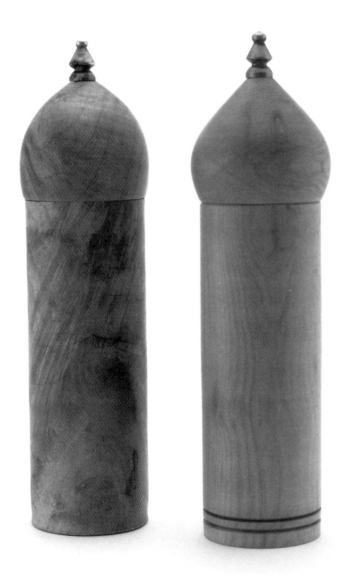

Pepper mills, 7¾ in. (195mm) tall
by 2⅛ in. (55mm) in diameter.

A mill for grinding peppercorns or sea salt is a popular project for turners. The one at left in the photo on the facing page, which I have enjoyed using for around 12 years, now looks a trifle stark and inelegant compared to its neighbor—I hope this indicates that I'm still managing to refine my forms. The addition of the lines at the base relieves the harshness of the cylinder, while the ogee curve on the top makes it look taller; in fact, both mills are the same height. I reckon this is an ideal size for a mill, and I wouldn't recommend making one larger for use as a personal pepper mill. While one the length of your arm might be fun in a restaurant, it isn't necessarily something you want to talk around at the breakfast table or twist over your eggs first thing in the morning.

Pepper mills are usually proffered as a drilling, rather than a turning, operation. But large-diameter drills are expensive: Two or three of these can equal the cost of a chuck. This has led to the practice of boring a comparatively narrow hole in a mill, typically half the diameter of the body, which seldom seems to hold a worthwhile amount of peppercorns. Instead of realizing the potential of the blank by enlarging the capacity, the classic mill design cuts into the wall thickness to create a long waist, very occasionally of some elegance. Increased capacity is generally achieved by making the mill taller, presumably to save buying a wider, more expensive bit. This would be an understandable solution in an amateur workshop, but not in a production situation, where tooling costs are to be expected. A better solution, if you want the capacity but only a few mills, is to turn out the inside. It takes a bit longer, but saves you buying a drill and challenges your improving skills.

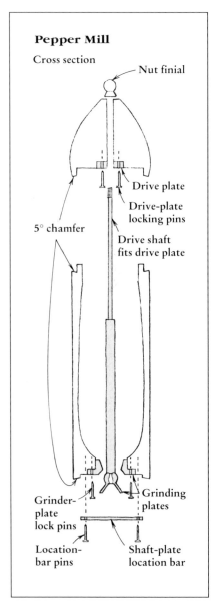

Pepper Mill

Cross section

Nut finial

Drive plate

Drive-plate locking pins

Drive shaft fits drive plate

5° chamfer

Grinder-plate lock pins

Grinding plates

Location-bar pins

Shaft-plate location bar

Mill mechanisms are available from woodturning specialty stores, ranging from 4 in. (100mm) to 18 in. (460mm) in length, but for a hand-turned mill choose a mechanism 8 in. (200mm) or shorter. The blank should be a well-seasoned, 2-in. (50mm) to 2¼-in. (55mm) square, ½ in. (13mm) longer than the mechanism. Lathe speed should be 1,500 rpm to 1,800 rpm.

Turning a Pepper Mill

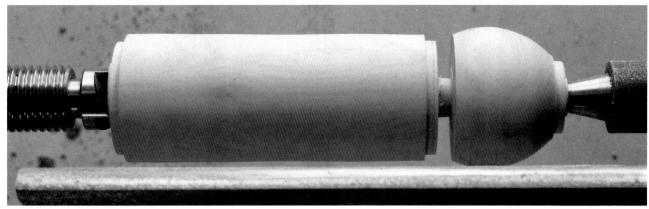

1. Develop the form and establish the proportions. I allow extra material on the lid for last-minute adjustments to accommodate the mechanism. Turn shoulders for the collet chuck on both ends of the body section, and on the top of the top. Turn the latter to fit a smaller collet (if you have one), so that there is less to remove during the final stages of shaping.

2. A pepper mill is made in much the same way as a box. Make the top first. As you true the blank, dish the face slightly to form a chamfered rim, which will seat nicely on the body.

3. I take a few cuts in about ¼ in. (6mm), using a ¼-in. (6mm) shallow gouge to prepare the way for a ½-in. (13mm) square-end scraper.

4. Turn the rabbet and recess for the mechanism's drive plate using a ½-in. (13mm) square-end scraper with the rest set at center height. If the rest is lower, you'll have to tilt the tool to have its left corner cut parallel to the axis. If the right corner touches the end grain, it'll catch and snap the tool down on to the rest, where it should have been all along. For a good fit, the recess should be cylindrical rather than tapered and ¼ in. (6mm) deep.

5. Measure the drive-plate recess. The drive plate is slotted so that the top and shaft rotate as one. Even though it will be pinned in place, the plate should fit snugly into the recess to prevent lateral drift. When the rabbet and recess are turned, use a drill equal in diameter to the mill-mechanism's shaft to bore a hole through the top. Then sand the rim, ensuring that it's chamfered inward, so that when the top sits on the base you have a neat joint. If it needs turning true, use a scraper very gently, or use a lighter-weight, small skew chisel on its side as a scraper with the grinding burr on top.

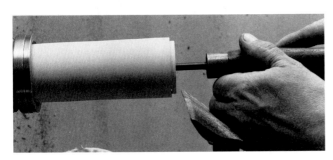

6. Mount the body section with the top in the collet so that you can turn the rabbets in the base. I start by drilling a hole right through the center using my depth drill. This eases the problems of cutting into end grain so far away from the chuck.

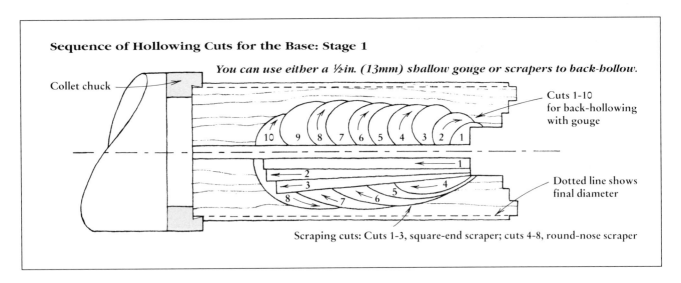

Sequence of Hollowing Cuts for the Base: Stage 1

You can use either a ½-in. (13mm) shallow gouge or scrapers to back-hollow.

Collet chuck

Cuts 1-10 for back-hollowing with gouge

10 9 8 7 6 5 4 3 2 1

1
2
3
8 7 6 5 4

Dotted line shows final diameter

Scraping cuts: Cuts 1-3, square-end scraper; cuts 4-8, round-nose scraper

7. Use a ¼-in. (6mm) square-end scraper to step out the recesses in 1⁄16-in. (1.5mm) steps. You can push the tool into end grain quite forcefully at the center, because the pressure is absorbed straight into the drive, but as you move away from the axis you must exercise greater caution. The leverage at this distance from the chuck is such that the slightest catch will knock the job off-center. Ease any pressure in the cut at the hint of chatter, and use your hand to support the wood, as shown on the bottom right photo on the facing page. Then chamfer the rim inward, so the mill will stand square.

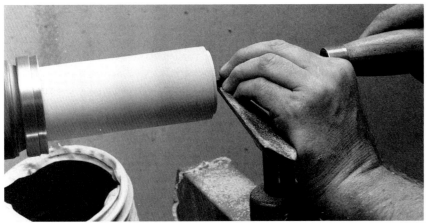

8. I use heavy-section scrapers to bore past the inner recess. I start with a square-end tool, then switch to a narrow round-nose scraper to work through the limited opening. The farther you work over the rest, the more the tools will want to catch—keep plenty of weight behind the tool. If you can hollow the mid-section of the body without damaging the inner recess, the final stages of hollowing will be much easier.

9. Reverse the body, so it is gripped around the base. Here I take a peeling cut, using the skew flat on the rest, to turn a taper over which the top will just fit.

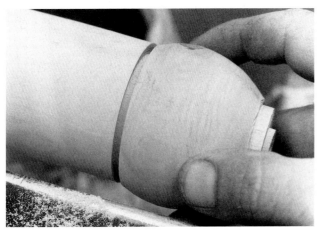

10. Don't fit the top properly at this stage—allow for the possibility of catches, which will shift the body in the chuck. If I fit the top, then knock the body off-center, I am unlikely ever to get a good fit. If the top fails to fit over the first taper you cut, turn the wider portion away so you have a cylinder the diameter of that rim. Then ease the tool around to cut another taper, working from a known position. If you simply reduce the diameter of the taper, you have no means of knowing by how much.

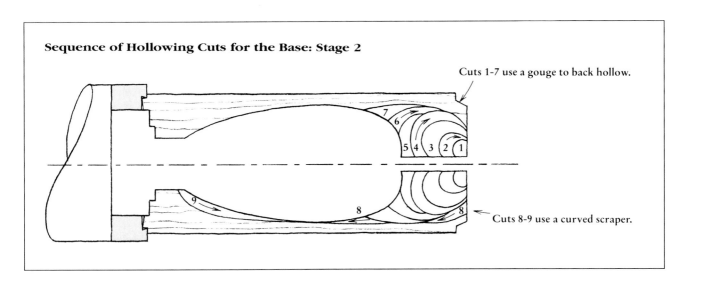

Sequence of Hollowing Cuts for the Base: Stage 2

Cuts 1-7 use a gouge to back hollow.

Cuts 8-9 use a curved scraper.

11. I start to hollow the end grain using the back-hollowing technique for speed. I use a ½-in. (13mm) gouge rolled over and cutting on the far side of center, meeting the wood as it comes up.

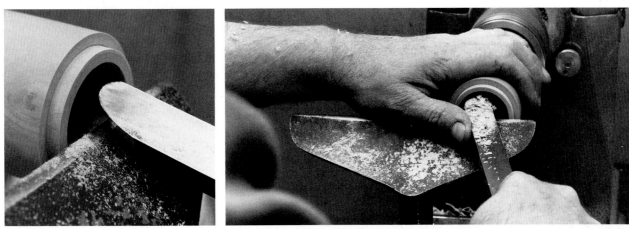

12. I remove the remainder of the inside with a heavy long-and-strong ¾-in. (20mm) round-nose scraper, but use no more than ¼ in. (6mm) of the edge at one time. I keep my hand on the wood to limit chatter and vibration. All my round scrapers are ground with a long left curve on the edge, because I always work inboard on the lathe and have no use for a long right-hand edge.

13. Before fitting the top, true up the taper. Use the long point of the skew to chamfer the shoulder inward, so the joint between top and base is a clean, definite line (the top is already chamfered). An alternative method is to scrape this shoulder, keeping the skew flat on the rest but using the left side of the bevel, which has enough burr from the grinding to do the job. I always touch up the edge of the skew on an 80-grit wheel for this cut, but only on one side, so that I have a slight burr on top of the edge.

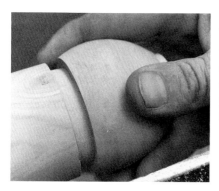

14. Test fit the top by holding it gently over the spinning body. This burnishes the taper and indicates exactly where the top fits. The top needs to fit tightly because you still have to refine the form, so turn the taper down to a cylinder a fraction over this diameter. I find the most accurate, safest way to do this is to keep the tool flat on the rest and ease the long point to the left into the wood, stopping to test the fit frequently. If you overcut, use a cloth to pad out the shoulder.

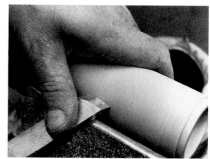

16. If you run into twisted grain or a knot and find that you can't get a reasonable surface from a shear cut, try a delicate peeling cut. It won't be as smooth as a sheared surface, but it will be in the right place and easily sanded smooth. You can see from the dust on the bevel that I use only about ¼ in. (6mm) of the edge. Any more can lead to a catch, but this is unlikely if the skew edge is curved.

15. Use calipers and a parting tool to establish the final diameter of the body (as with the rolling pin on p. 22). A skew chisel smooths the cylinder to that diameter.

17. Fit the top and measure the total length of the mill to see what adjustments need to be made, then mark this on the top.

18. I turn away the bulk of the waste using a ¼-in. (6mm) shallow gouge, and I support the job just in case the top flies off. Note how my left thumb acts as a fulcrum on the rest.

19. Final cuts are taken with the skew. The top is dished slightly so that the finial, which keeps the mill together, seats properly. This done, sand and polish what you can reach, which is all except the foot and base in the chuck. Remove the top when you sand the body; otherwise, there's a tendency to lose the form toward the shoulder on which the top sits.

20. Turn or sand the flange so that the top can rotate freely, but without rattling around. Turning is more accurate than sanding, but be sure to take only fine dust as you ease the tool in. If you're nervous, definitely sand, although if you've gotten this far the turning should be well within your capabilities.

21. Finally, mount the whole mill between centers, using a tapered plug at the drive end and padding out the flange with tissue paper so the lid fits tightly. Turn or sand away the chuck marks at the base, and finish. I later found the body a bit stark, so I rechucked the body between centers and cut in decorative grooves, as you can see in the photo on p. 106.

4. Facework

Facework means that the fibers of the wood rotate at right angles to the lathe axis. To shear cut the wood—that is, to cut each fiber when it is supported by another below or behind—you will generally work from smaller diameter to larger diameter on the outside of the job, and from larger to smaller on the inside.

The tools for facework are gouges and scrapers. The skew chisel is used only rarely, for scraping in odd corners. Roughing cuts are best made with gouges rather than scrapers, which are slow, inelegant and rather prosaic to use by comparison. Until the early 1980s, the available gouges were either deep fluted (sold as bowl gouges) or shallow (sold as spindle gouges). In general, each was used as the name suggested. A number of half-round gouges, which are a compromise between the other two, are now available. They're enjoyable to use and among my favorite tools.

Hollowing the inside of any bowl form—such as the hollow vessel shown on p. 150—demands a substantial tool with the bulk to withstand flexing when the cut is made some distance from the rest. The deep-fluted long-and-strong gouge is the supreme tool for the job. Half-round gouges are also excellent for hollowing, but are marginally less substantial than a deep-fluted tool of similar diameter. The shallow gouges can be used similarly, but because they are designed for centerwork use, where cutting is always near the rest, they have even less bulk. Nor can the relatively flat curved flute of the shallow gouge be ground to offer a cutting capacity equal to the deeper-fluted tools.

For outside roughing cuts it's a different story. Here I favor shallow or half-round gouges, because the shavings never jam in the flute, as they can with a deep-fluted gouge if you use your upper hand to deflect the shavings. It's never a major problem, but it puts avoidable hiccups into the work flow. By extending the normal fingernail-ground edge to a slightly longer curve, you can make sweeping scraping cuts to remove shavings as wide as the tool. That's difficult to beat for sheer bravado and exhilaration, but such showmanship is rather wasteful of timber.

I use mostly scrapers and shear-scraping techniques with gouges for finishing cuts. Often you can improve even the best of shearing back cuts from the gouge.

The grips are similar to those used in the centerwork projects. To reiterate, most problems stem from pushing the tool too hard against the wood as you cut, and against the axis as well. Remember, big shavings come from a sharp tool held at the optimum angle, not from force.

If you've practiced the beads and can turn a set of identical grooves on a meat-basher head (see pp. 32-34) with few problems, you should find the remaining projects in this book relatively easy.

Most of the projects in this chapter require stable material, ideally from quartersawn boards. These are easily identified on the end grain, where you'll see the growth rings running parallel to the board edges, as shown at A in the drawing on the facing page. Wood is rarely as dry as lumberyards like to think, and "dry" is rarely dry enough at the point of purchase. And wood goes on moving with the seasons, too. It's one of its little foibles (and attractions). If you want utter stability in your turning projects, use plastics or take up metal turning. Quartersawn boards will shrink in width, but you'll have minimal problems with warping. If you turn a trivet or tray from unseasoned timber it can become slightly oval, which is appealing, although chances are that the end grain will split. Not my ideal, but it would offer an opportunity to experiment with detailing the defects.

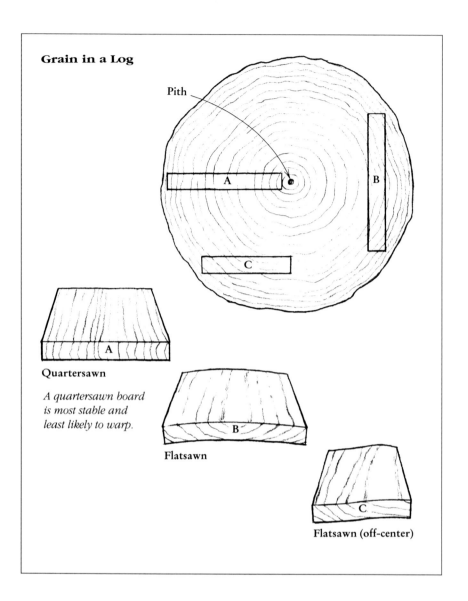

Grain in a Log

Pith

A

B

C

A

Quartersawn

A quartersawn board is most stable and least likely to warp.

B

Flatsawn

C

Flatsawn (off-center)

If you have trouble obtaining wide seasoned boards or dry blanks, you will have to join narrower boards to get the widths you want. If you lack the equipment or expertise to do this, employ a local cabinetmaker to do the job, using quartersawn material. Although this could be expensive, laminations must be executed well if the disc is to stay whole on the lathe—don't risk serious injury for the sake of a few dollars.

Boards

Cutting boards, 10 in. (255mm) in
diameter by 1⅛ in. (30mm) thick.

I use the word "board" loosely. Boards can be used for cutting just about anything, for serving cheese, and as trivets, place mats or platters.

You need to be able to pick up such a practical object, so the edge of a board needs special consideration. If you leave at least ⅝ in. (15mm) of space beneath the rim to accommodate fingers, even a large board will be easy to lift, especially if the rim is wide or has a bead or recess. In the drawing at right, the first two rims are more suited to small diameters and double-sided use. A cove or groove is often featured just inside the rim of the upper face, theoretically to catch meat juices or crumbs. Juices? Perhaps. Crumbs? Definitely not. In fact, this classic feature is really a decorative device to highlight the rim on an otherwise stark form.

Boards provide good exercise in turning a flat surface. They are easily tested against a straightedge, which will give you something precise to aim for. For the blank, choose a seasoned disc about 10 in. (250mm) to 12 in. (305mm) in diameter and 1¼ in. (32mm) thick. For stability and minimal warping, the blank should come from a quartersawn board (see the drawing on p. 117).

Board Edge Profiles

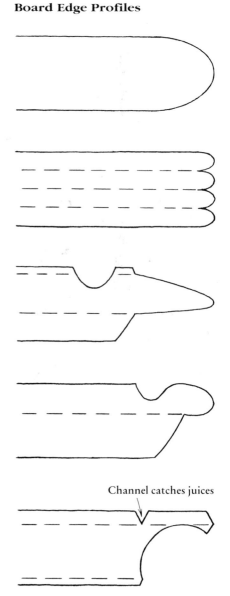

Channel catches juices

There are several ways to fix the blank to the lathe. The problem, if you are going to turn the base, is how to hold the blank initially without messing up the top surface. You can use a large faceplate, which allows you to grip the blank with screws near the rim. This allows you to turn a rabbet in the base for a collet chuck, which, to the layman's eye, is rather decorative, but the board will have only one cutting surface. You eliminate the screw holes on the top face as you turn a decorative rim. I used this method when I first started turning, creating a large-diameter faceplate by screwing a 14-in. (355mm) disc to a 6-in. (150mm) faceplate, which was the largest I had. Alternatively, you can use hot glue instead of screws, and stick the blank to your faceplate. For this, plane or sand one face of the blank flat and turn the board on one fixing. The finished board is easily pried away once the glue is warmed. I use a knife heated in a gas-torch flame.

My preferred method of attachment, mainly for the speed of production, is a screw chuck. The single center screw hole is obscured with a decorative plug or three, as shown in the bottom right photo on p. 123. A bowed or uneven face should be planed or sanded flat for a good grip. The blank should be secure on a ½-in. (13mm) long screw.

The board shown in the photo essay was turned with the lathe running at 1,200 rpm, which I think is fast enough. Many professionals turn at much higher speeds, but I find I get there about as fast with less dust and stress.

The finish required on chopping boards does not have to be perfectly smooth. In production, I found that boards finished with 120-grit sandpaper and oiled always sold more readily than smoother, more highly polished ones. People don't want to mess up a highly polished surface, so aim for a reasonably smooth, matte surface that fulfills the general idea of what is fit for the purpose.

Turning a Board

1. True the side of the blank first, making sure to stand out of the firing line in case the disc flies off. I favor a ½-in. (13mm) long-and-strong shallow or half-round gouge for exterior roughing rather than a deep-fluted tool, because the open shape of the former gives the shavings more room to fly away.

2. If you keep your upper hand nearer the edge of the tool, you can allow the shavings to build up a bit, which will offer protection against the odd splinter. It is in this situation that a deep-fluted tool can jam with shavings.

3. Cut in from each face so as not to split the rim fibers away. Note that the tool is rolled into the cut. If held with the top flat, the tool will catch. If the board has to be a precise thickness, mark this now, measuring from the base rim. True this rim before you measure.

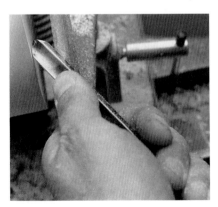

4. The three fingers of my upper hand squeeze the edge of a shallow ½-in. (13mm) gouge into the wood to establish a smooth surface. It is against this surface that the bevel rides for a shearing cut back to the center. It also shows how much material I have to work with.

5. I use the same gouge to create the curve under the rim. To take a shearing cut (from the center outward on external surfaces), the tool has to be tilted up and pulled toward the rim under tight control. Here my fingers and thumb are in opposition, setting up the tension that is controlled by my lower hand. While the rest supports the tool, the fulcrum is on my forefinger as the tool sweeps to the right.

6. The result should be a smooth surface, though it's not often as good as this.

7. To true the top face, take a shearing cut into the center from the rim. Check for flatness using a steel rule held firmly against the moving surface; bumps will be burnished, enabling you to see the sections that need attention. The gouge will leave tiny ridges, which will sand away easily.

8. You can often get a much smoother surface by stroking the surface with a shearing scrape. For this I use my arrowhead scraper tilted on its bottom left corner so that the slightly curved edge lies at about 30° above the horizontal. The tool lies at 45° to the wood surface, but the extremely light pressure on the edge is unlikely to snap it down. The rest is set at 90° to the axis. The tool is held firmly in position as it is pulled from the center to the rim, so that the cutting edge remains an even distance from the rest. The intent is to move the tool evenly in a straight line along the rest regardless of what's there, be it wood or space. An uneven surface will require a number of passes with the tool, and you should test the surface with the straightedge after each pass.

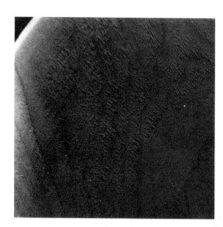

9. The outer portion of this celery-top pine board has been turned using a gouge, and the small ridges are visible across the slightly torn grain. Eighty-grit abrasive will soon smooth such a surface, but the shearing scrape is more elegant and leaves the surface smoother, as seen around the eye figure in the grain. Another pass should remove the flatter ridges left by the shearing scrape.

10. To create the rim detail, cut a series of small arcs with a ¼-in. (6mm) gouge. Sand these arcs and the underside before the top face, so as not to lose the crisp edge of the top rim.

11. Back the abrasive with a sanding block and check frequently for a center bump. To remove this bump, stop the lathe and hand sand, rotating the job with your left hand.

12. With the job almost completed, the penultimate task is to block out the screw hole with a decorative insert. I secure these with cyanoacrylate super glue for speed. Finally, I sand the base flat on the belt sander.

13. When you insert plugs to cover the screw holes you create another work surface, so you can use the board either way up.

Design Variations

Lazy Susan, 22 in. (560mm) in diameter; Alan Cantor, Canberra, Australia. This beautifully simple revolving tray consists of a top mounted on a bearing fixed to a base. It allows a number of people to help themselves at a large table where passing things around could be a problem. Bearings are readily available from stores that stock woodturning accessories.

A stool is little more than a bread board on legs—babies should receive one at birth to see them through life. During infancy, a stool serves as a table, seat and climbing aid. In the middle decades, it makes an ideal low table for drinks or, since it is basically a milking stool, for groping for the udders of cows or goats if you do that sort of thing. And then it's just the right footstool height for old age. If it survives all that, you've got an heirloom for subsequent generations. In a low stool, the leg angle should be around 15° off horizontal. The feet can cause problems. A spherical end (A in the drawing below) will save you having to cut them accurately. For a flat end (B) draw a line parallel to the surface it's standing on, using a scrap of wood as a gauge, as at C, and cut away the waste to the line.

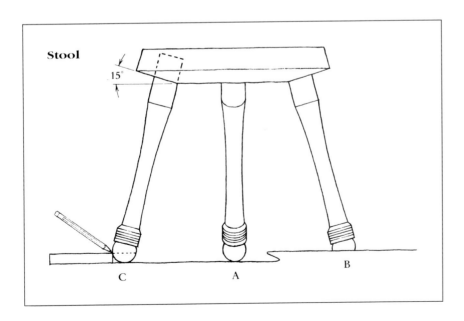

Stool

15°

C   A   B

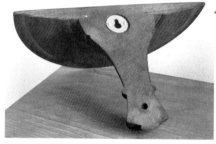

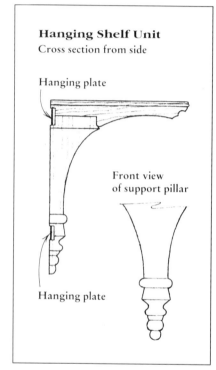

Hanging Shelf Unit
Cross section from side

Hanging plate

Front view
of support pillar

Hanging plate

This shelf unit is made up of a spindle inserted into a recess in the base of a board. My bandsaw has a depth of cut that allows me to assemble and glue the parts before cutting them in half with the flat top face down on the saw table. If your saw lacks this depth of cut, split the top and spindle separately, then join the parts. (See p. 143 for a jigging spindle for splitting and drilling.) I flatten the back on a disc or belt sander, then drill the holes for the hanging plates. In the example shown, I use a simple hole for the vertical alignment pin rather than a hanging plate. The set of nesting boxes was made by my brother, Simon Raffan.

In several parts of the world there is a strong tradition of carved decoration around a wide rim; biblical texts and wheat ears seem to be the most popular and appropriate.

Trivets

Trivet, 9½ in. (240mm) in diameter
by ⅝ in. (15mm) thick.

A trivet is a stand for hot kettles, pots, pans, irons or anything else that might mark a surface you want protected. As a project, it makes a fine bead-cutting exercise on a face with cross grain, producing an article never regarded as useful until you have one (then you wonder how you ever managed without it).

When you first make trivets, try to turn even beads or coves. The advantage of a project like this is that you can repeat tool movements time and again, so that you begin to do them automatically. Once you can turn a set of even shapes, you can move on to little compound curves or combinations of beads and coves. The idea is to provide a series of ridges for the pot to stand on while the heat is dissipated in the air pockets between. Convenient sizes range from 3 in. (75mm) in diameter by ³⁄₁₆ in. (5mm) thick for coffee mugs, to 12 in. (305mm) in diameter by 1 in. (25mm) thick for hot and heavy casseroles.

For early attempts, the blank should be at least ⅝ in. (15mm) thick, with a diameter of around 8 in. (200mm). The blank can be held on a short center screw—one that is ⅜ in. (9mm) should grip well enough if the backing plate is at least 3 in. (75mm) in diameter. Later the hole can be plugged like the boards on p. 123. A good alternative is to sand the base flat, then use hot glue or double-sided tape to stick the blank onto the standard faceplate supplied with every lathe. I prefer hot glue, because you need only a bit of heat from a hot knife or heat gun to warm the adhesive and release the job.

Lathe speed should not exceed 1,200 rpm. True up the disc so the surface is flat, just like a board, then use a ¼-in. (6mm) shallow gouge to cut a series of grooves into the face. The centrifugal forces want to throw the tool away from center, so you need a grip that prevents the tool from kicking back. In each of the following photos, you can see that I keep my finger firmly on the rest to act as a stop, as well as a fulcrum, as the edge pivots into the wood.

Turning a Trivet

1. Only when the face is turned truly flat (you can test this with a straightedge) do you begin to cut the grooves. Start with the gouge angled up about 45°, riding on the bevel with the edge clear of the wood.

2. By raising the handle, you pivot the nose of the gouge forward through an arc into the wood. The moment the tip of the tool is in the wood you have a shoulder on which the bevel can ride, giving you all the control you need over the edge.

3. Now pivot the edge in to cut the right side of the groove. Here my forefinger hooks over the top of the blade to prevent any kickback toward the center. My lower hand forces the blade against my second finger (acting as a stop on the right), setting up a grip of tension.

4. At the bottom of the groove, roll the tool onto its side and hold it firmly. This means absolutely still—no longer pushing or arcing into the wood. The point will define the bottom of the groove, while the curve of the lower edge will scrape along the left side of the groove.

5. Cut a second groove to create a bead. The gouge starts off riding on the right shoulder of the groove you've just cut, with the tool angled up about 45° and the edge clear of the wood. You then pivot the edge forward into the wood, just as on the first cut.

6. Cut the right side of the second groove, repeating the actions of the first right-side cut.

7. I take tiny sweeping cuts with the gouge nose to remove the small facets and thereby round the bead, but I could just as easily remove these by sanding with 100-grit to 120-grit abrasive.

8. Continue cutting grooves until you have a faceful. On the second bead from center, just above the rest, the grain tore out. This sanded away, but I could have turned a cove. It is important that the top of each bead be in the same plane, so that anything set on the trivet sits firmly without rocking. If the surface has become uneven during turning, use 80-grit to 100-grit abrasive on a sanding block to true the top of the beads flat, then sand the shoulders round.

9. This 1-in. (25mm) thick trivet was mounted first on a screw chuck, then reversed onto the contracting collar of the Raffan collet chuck. The hole left from the first fixing is turned out and decorated with grooves.

Design Variations

Wall piece, 41 in. (1,040mm) in diameter; Vic Wood, Melbourne, Australia. This is pure sculpture, with no pretensions to being even vaguely practical. If you have a spectacular piece of wood you want to admire and not chance to the rigors of daily abuse, a wall piece is a good idea, and certainly a better design solution than some of those mini-footed platters that lurk in so many craft galleries.

Tasmanian myrtle bread-crock lid; Simon Raffan, Lilydale, Tasmania, Australia.

This weed pot is turned on both sides, with a small section of the rim cut away to provide a flat surface so that it can stand on edge. By drilling a hole in this base, you can add extra weight for stability. Here I drilled a hole through the center of an 8-in. (200mm) diameter, 2-in. (50mm) thick disc, which allowed me to turn each face with the blank mounted on the screw center. Finally, the center was turned with the piece mounted into a jam-fit chuck.

Bottle Coasters

Bottle coaster, 4⅛ in. (105mm) in diameter by 1¾ in. (45mm) tall.

On every bowl with the grain running across the blank you will encounter the end grain four times—twice inside, twice outside. One powerful reason for having bowls with curved profiles is that the end grain is easier to cut. The most difficult end grain to cut cleanly is on small-diameter cylinders, so here is a project which is just that. In addition, the bottom inside needs to be flat, but I have followed the tradition established in wood-based Victorian silver-plate coasters by decorating that surface with beads.

Coasters tend to be associated with wine bottles or decanters, their purpose being to protect polished tables from alcohol carelessly spilled by the tipsy. But you could as well have one to upgrade the image of a milk carton on the breakfast table, a flower pot or a ceramic vase.

For the blank, choose well-seasoned wood 2 in. (50mm) thick and 4½ in. (115mm) to 5 in. (125mm) in diameter, depending on the size of the bottle. Lathe speed is 1,200 rpm to 1,500 rpm.

Profiles for Coasters

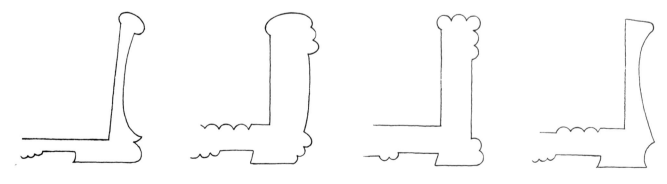

Turning a Bottle Coaster

1. I turn the outside first, truing the blank to a cylinder using the tool angled upward about 10° and at about 45° to the surface—the precise angle is dictated by the angle of your bevel. On this ½-in. (13mm) shallow gouge, the bevel is about 30° to the flute.

2. The base is turned to accept an expanding collet, then decorated to disguise that fact. This is a characteristic surface to aim for off the tool. The few feathers of fiber at the base of the beads will sand away with 180-grit abrasive, though I start with 100-grit to take the facets off the beads faster.

3. With the job reversed and mounted on the expanding jaws of the Raffan collet chuck for completion, I take a series of shearing cuts. These start ½ in. (13mm) in from the rim and end the same distance from the base, shaping the center rabbet while leaving a ring of material at top and bottom for beading.

4. Here the point of the gouge is pivoted in to cut the base of the upper bead while roughing the rabbet. Note how my fingers and thumb oppose one another as they squeeze around the tool, which is pulled onto the rest by my forefinger hooked under the rest. The bevel is aligned in the direction I'm cutting, and the tool is on its side.

5. As you cut into the base of the cove, pivot the tool sideways to bring the point of cut onto the nose, and roll the tool to avoid catching the lower edge.

6. To cut the left shoulder, I pivot the gouge nose into the wood. Then I mirror the cut just made at the base of the upper bead. Take similar pivotal cuts to create a double bead on the lower ring of material.

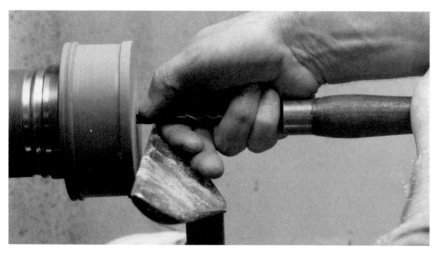

7. When the outside is ready for sanding, use a depth drill to drill the depth hole, allowing for a ½-in. (13mm) thick base.

8. Normally you would use a deep-fluted gouge to rough turn the inside, but I suggest you use a scraper all the way for practice. It's almost as fast, probably faster if the wood is really hard, but the main reason is to get the feel of what you can do with a scraper. Here I use about half the edge of a ¾-in. (19mm) square-end tool to cut in a series of steps. The tool edge is actually slightly curved back from the left corner, which eases the task of turning the flat surface at the bottom of the recess. If you are using a collet chuck, experiment with a range of pressures as you cut and see what happens. If you use excessive force, the job will probably slip on the collet rather than come off. Either way you can relocate it on the collet. Don't try this using a screw center, because you will not be able to screw the job back on when it comes loose.

9. The inner wall is best finished using the round nose of the ¼-in. (6mm) shallow gouge. The surface off the gouge (in front of the rim) is superior to that left by the sharp corner of the scraper.

10. I use the corners of a ½-in. (13mm) square-end scraper to turn the decorative grooves in the base. Always regrind the tool before taking such finishing cuts so that the corners are as sharp as possible. Here you could use a skew chisel's long point with the tool flat on the rest as a scraper.

Design Variations

Paperweights, about 4 in. (100mm) in diameter. Paperweights are good for developing control of the gouge as you develop an eye for cutting the forms of simple shapes, but they can be as difficult as you want to make them. They're good, too, for using up the odd scraps and offcuts from large bowls. To mount them, I drill a 2-in. (50mm) hole in the base and jam the blank onto a very shallow taper for turning. When the form is turned and sanded, I insert a flattened lead fishing weight in the hole and then a decorative plug. Finally the base is flattened on a sander, or mounted in a jam-fit chuck for turning to a nice rounded form that can be used either way up.

These candle holders were turned from very uncompromising-looking bowl-blank offcuts held initially on a screw chuck while I turned the underside and base to fit my collet chuck. I sanded the sides smooth after the turning was completed and left all waxing, oiling and polishing until last, rather than doing it piecemeal on the lathe.

Candle Holders

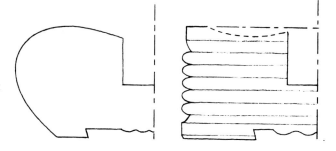

Trays

Tray, 16 in. (405mm) in diameter.

A tray is for offering and presenting, but the real challenge is aesthetic. The rim should provide a frame for the food, drinking glasses or calling cards, while defining the serviceable area they might occupy. Since a tray should be easy to pick up, the rim should also encourage a firm grip. The base should be concave rather than flat, so that if the tray warps slightly you can flatten just the rim on a belt sander, or rechuck it to turn the rim if you use a collet chuck. For stability, the base should also be nearly as wide **as the** working area.

I define a tray as having a flat internal surface, compared to platters, which tend to be curved—neither should present any problems once you can turn a flat board. I avoid having the flat surface curve up to the rim, because that's where glasses always seem to end up wobbling and spilling. Since the end grain often requires harder sanding, there is also a tendency during sanding to develop a dip in the curve, which mars the flow of the line and jars your sense of touch. The simplest solution is to detail the transition with a small step.

The blank should be a well-seasoned disc 12 in. (305mm) to 14 in. (355mm) in diameter and 1¼ in. (32mm) to 1½ in. (38mm) thick. Hold the blank on a screw chuck for the back to be turned, but be careful not to drill the hole too deep. A wide backing plate of 6 in. (150mm) to 8 in. (200mm) will increase the friction and therefore the grip, allowing you to use a shorter screw than those supplied on commercial chucks. Use a disc to reduce the length of the screw to ⁵⁄₁₆ in. (11mm)..

Run the lathe no faster than 1,200 rpm. If the blank is off-balance with uneven grain, select a lower speed. Always err on the side of caution when first starting the lathe.

Tray Profiles

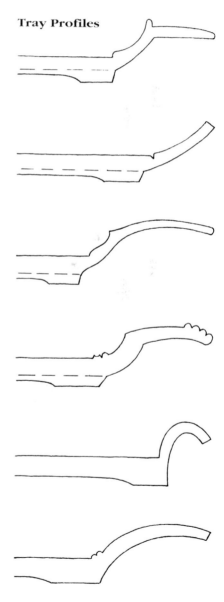

139

Turning a Tray

1. Above left: True the disc sides and base, then dish the base slightly. I smooth the base here using a scraper flat to cut minuscule shavings, before checking the surface with a rule.

2. Above right: Lay out the collet diameter using dividers, and cut a dovetailed rabbet. I have a small skew scraper just for this job, ground from an old carving skew chisel. Keep your odd lengths of old chisels, gouges and scrapers for such shop-made tools. If you are using the screw chuck for the second fixing, use the freehand drilling technique shown on p. 109, but carefully, so as not to go too deep. Be aware that the drill can suddenly pull into the wood.

3. Don't forget to check that the collet fits. Note that you don't need the whole depth of the collet jaw for a good grip — ⅛ in. (3mm) should be sufficient here.

4. Keep as much material in the base as the collet will allow, but make it decorative. I use the ¼-in. (6mm) shallow gouge for all such small bead work, bringing in the edge in a series of little arcs for the beads (as for the trivet on pp. 129-130), but moving the tool forward for the final curve into the center. Here the recess is just about ready for sanding.

5. Turn the underside of the rim, but don't sand the surface in case you need to true it or alter the form later. Remember to allow a margin for error.

7. Here the basic form is roughed out. The surface is not that clean, but I prefer speed to finesse at this stage. The rim is reduced, but I retain enough bulk to keep my design options open and a stiffening rim around the thinner flat section until that's finished.

6. Rechuck the tray for hollowing. Before you turn away the center, increase the center-hole depth, leaving a thickness of at least ⅝ in. (16mm) across the base. Chances are that your screw hole will be just about right. An alternative to having one depth hole at the center is to sink several, using a Forstner bit with no central spur in a drill press. The advantage of this is that you can turn to the bottom of the holes spread across the surface, speeding up the basic turning. However, you do reduce your options should you run into some defect or interesting grain pattern.

8. I use my arrowhead scraper to smooth the flat working surface of the tray. In this case I'm using just the corner where the dust is.

9. I check the surface using my four-straightedges-in-one, which I made on the belt sander.

10. I swing the tool around to use the point to clean out the corner.

11. The working surface is ready for sanding. You can see a little wall, which will become the bead that marks the transition from flat surface to rim.

12. To minimize flex, equalize the tool pressure with your hand on the underside of the rim. Sand the underside of the rim a bit, because a smoother surface will generate less frictional heat on your fingers. All the ½-in. (13mm) gouge needs in this position is a backstop to prevent kickback. There's no need to have your fingers on the side of the tool facing center. The shaving comes off the rounded nose of the tool, which is rolled onto its side to detail the corner at the base of the rough bead, as on the trivet.

13. To establish the overall proportion of the bead, I ease the edge in to turn away the top of the bead by pivoting the tool on the bevel shoulder that rides on the freshly cut rim. This is far more controlled than pivoting the tool on the rest so that the edge arcs in from space.

14. Here I create a double bead using the ¼-in. (6mm) shallow gouge. I start with the bevel riding on the outer rim of the roughed bead, then pivot the edge into the center, rolling the tool on its side to avoid a catch. The shaving comes off the right side of the rounded nose. When I've cut deeply enough, I hold the tool in position for a couple of seconds, so that the lower right portion of the edge scrapes the other side of the groove being made. I find this technique of cutting with the point, then resting the tool in position while the lower section of the blade scrapes, to be useful in all detailing situations. There must be only minimal tool pressure against the wood.

15. As I take a similar cut from the other side, I must adjust my upper grip. Now my little finger acts as a stop to prevent kickback, while the other fingers pull the tool against that stop as well as against the pressure of my lower hand on the handle. Use variations of these cuts to take little arcs to round the beads.

16. For extra definition at the base of the bead, I use the long point of the skew chisel as I would for cutting a groove on a spindle. The grain alignment varies as the wood rotates, which tends to kick the tool sideways, so the tool needs to be under particularly tight control. Use the point only to make a line where the bead sits on the curve of the rim.

17. Sanding proceeds as with a board (see p. 123), using a block to maintain the flat surface.

Design Variations

Side table, 17¾ in. (450mm) in diameter by 15¾ in. (240mm) high. The top was turned on a center screw chuck from a blank of laminated small-section boards, with the hole plugged as in the board on p. 123. The rim (a ring from the bowl blank on p. 158) improves the visual impact of the joined boards. To drill holes accurately in a leg for the rails, draw the angles on the spindle end, then hold the spindle in a V-jig that is precisely aligned with the drill (see the drawing below). Here the holes are for a three-legged table.

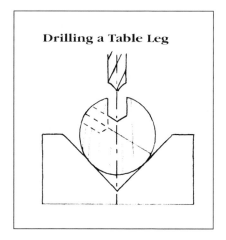

Drilling a Table Leg

Hand Mirrors

Hand mirror, 4⅛ in. (105mm)
in diameter.

This small hand mirror, which measures about 4 in. (100mm) in diameter, is ideal for use in a purse, though it needs to live in a soft leather pouch to protect the glass from scratching. The 3-in. (75mm) diameter glass is sandwiched between the front and back, so that the reflective surface becomes a pool of light overlaid by a frame, rather than the insert with a definable edge it would be if merely stuck into a rabbet. This project is a trifle finicky. The back insert is turned in one operation, the frame is rechucked two or three times, then the whole assembly is mounted to finish the back.

An object as personal as a hand mirror should not have sharp edges, but rounded sensual curves and subtle ridges. It must be a joy to handle; its keeper should be reluctant to put it away after use. It must be slim for ease of handling and carrying, so aim for the finished project to be between ¼ in. (6mm) and ⅜ in. (10mm) thick. Use well-seasoned wood known for its stability and reluctance to split. The casuarina used here was a bad choice for the frame since it splits easily, but would have been fine for the back insert. You will need two blanks, each with the grain running across the face. For a 3-in. (75mm) glass, the disc for the frame should be 4¼ in. (110mm) in diameter and ⅜ in. (10mm) thick. The back-insert blank is 3½ in. (90mm) in diameter and ³⁄₁₆ in. (5mm) thick. Lathe speed should be between 1,800 rpm and 2,100 rpm.

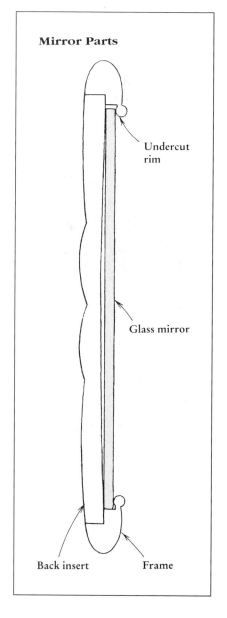

Mirror Parts

Undercut rim

Glass mirror

Back insert   Frame

Turning a Hand Mirror

1. Attach a waste block to each blank. Here I use three blobs of hot glue, which is quick, secure and inexpensive. This waste block already fits my collet chuck since it is the stub of a scoop blank. It pays to keep any stub remaining in your chuck after a job for later use as a waste block or jam-fit chuck. If you're working off a screw chuck, you'll need a deeper waste block to accommodate the screw.

2. Turn the back insert, which will locate the mirror as well as provide decoration. Make a straight-sided disc ¼ in. (6mm) larger than the diameter of the glass. The face should be flat or slightly concave to locate the glass satisfactorily; a convex face will bear against the center of the glass, inviting breakage, so check the surface with a straightedge. Don't part off the disc from the waste block — later on, when assembling the parts of the mirror, the block will function as a handy knob. Just set the back aside while completing the frame.

3. Turn the frame blank true. This will be the top of the frame, so mark a diameter about ¼ in. (6mm) less than the glass.

4. Use a parting tool to part in parallel to the axis.

5. Use a ¼-in. (6mm) shallow gouge to turn the rim profile, which is similar to that on a breadboard.

6. The inner rim will look better rounded but needs attacking from both sides. I work the curve around as far as I can to the underside using the side of the skew bevel for a light scraping cut. To avoid a catch, you need to tilt the tool onto its lower left corner, so be sure to keep the point and cutting edge clear of the bottom of the rabbet.

7. Finish turning the outer rim and the curve to the back. The frame has to be sanded and waxed at this stage if you want to remount it into a jam chuck for tuning the back, which is the safest method.

8. Use the long point of the skew chisel to cut the frame free. If you cut through as near parallel to the axis as possible, you should avoid dangerous sharp edges, which means you can let the frame spin off into your fingers. There are two options for chucking the frame section so that you can turn the rabbets for the glass and the back insert. Most secure is a jam-fit chuck, which encloses the frame, but since you can't get at the outer rim, you'll have to fair the curve on the back once the mirror is assembled. If you mount the frame over a taper, the frame's bearing surface is the inner rim. This needs more work anyway and soon reduces to less than 1/16 in. (1½mm), demanding a very light touch with the tools and not the slightest snick of a catch. In the end, I find it handy to have both types of chuck at my disposal.

9. The fibers left from the parting cut are most accessible if the frame is mounted in a jam-fit chuck. The wood of the chuck should be softer than that of the frame, to lessen possible damage to the frame rim. I use a ½-in. (13mm) square-end scraper to turn the rabbets for the glass and back insert and to complete the inner-rim curve. Chamfer the rim to ensure a precise line of contact on the glass, as shown in the drawing on p. 145. The rabbet for the glass should be slightly oversize to allow for any movement in the wood. The glass must fit flush with, or proud of, the top of the rabbet. Lever the frame from the chuck to check the inner rim/glass contact.

10. I prefer to use the skew chisel's long point as a scraper for making microadjustments to the diameter and to clean out the corners, because it is a lighter tool than the heavier section scrapers. I can feel the cut.

11. The back insert should be able to rotate in the rabbet, but not be loose enough to move from side to side. The waste-block knob means you shouldn't have to take the frame from the chuck to remove the insert each time you test the fit.

12. Remove the frame and assemble the parts. I use hot glue to hold the glass in place because it's thick and rubbery and can accommodate some movement in the wood.

13. For speed I use cyanoacrylate super glue to fix the back in place. Make sure that the grain aligns with the grain on the frame, so that when the woods move they do so together rather than in opposition. Now you'll appreciate the retention of the waste block as a knob. Remove it with a thin hot knife if you intend to reuse it, or turn it away with a small gouge.

14. On most very hard woods—this is African blackwood—I get the cleanest surface from a scraper. When using a jam chuck, I favor a lightweight tool lying back at an angle to the wood. Rather than grind a skew-end scraper, I use my trusty ½-in. (13mm) skew as a scraper yet again. When I grind it, I do the lower bevel last, so that the burr works similarly to that on a more conventional scraper.

15. If you can't pry the job from the chuck, either tap the back with something heavy like the lathe wrench or even a hammer, or tap the rim on a firm surface.

Hollow Vessels

Hollow vessel, 8⅝ in. (220mm) in diameter by 4 in. (100mm) tall.

In the 1980s, the world of woodturning saw the phenomenon of the hollow vessel. Masters of the genre have vied to produce increasingly larger and thinner vessels hollowed through ever smaller openings. The technical virtuosity of such pieces will always be astounding, as will be the amount of truly wonderful timber turned from within many of these these vessels that has gone to waste.

The idea behind the technique I offer here is to take a lump of wood, cut it in two, extract the inside whole for the creation of some other object(s), then stick the two portions together again to look like one piece. It might demand less skill than conventional hollow turning, but it offers the opportunity to minimize waste. And now that timber is widely recognized as a rapidly diminishing resource, it is even more essential that we don't squander it. The fact that you make the maximum use of expensive wood bought with hard-earned cash is relevant for many of us, too.

The blank for the vessel shown was 9 in. (230mm) in diameter and 4¼ in. (110mm) thick. Regard the construction of the form as a fairly standard bowl with a flat lid stuck on. Lathe speed should be 800 rpm to 1,200 rpm.

Turning a Hollow Vessel

1. To ease the strain on my small 1-hp bandsaw, I cut away two corners, then stand the blank on the remaining flat side and cut the ½-in. (13mm) thick slab that will form the top of the vessel. Note that I adjust my grip on the blank when it's sawn halfway through, so that my left hand guides the blank from behind the blade. Alternatively, use a push stick and keep your fingers farther from danger. Small as it is, my Startrite bandsaw will cut 11½-in. (290mm) thick material. An alternative method of separation would be to cut in on each side of a square using a circular saw, then saw the rest by hand (which is actually quite quick) before cutting the discs. Or use a parting tool on the lathe.

2. To cut away the remaining corners, I pass both sections through the saw in their original alignment. This saves me from having to find the center of the base section. Then, keeping the blanks aligned, drill a hole at the center through the upper blank into the lower blank for the center-screw chuck.

3. Turn the underside of the top first. This will be glued to the top of a thin bowl—the body of the vessel. I use a ½ in. (13mm) square-end scraper to turn a rabbet on the rim of the top—the rabbet increases the surface area available for gluing and thereby the strength of the top-to-body joint. The rest of the face is shear cut with a shallow gouge. Check that the rim is flat using a straightedge to ensure a good joint. Although it will never be seen, I decorate the inside of the top and sand it. Only a very small finger will be able to reach inside the finished vessel to experience the surface (adults can't have all the fun).

Vessel Top-to-Bottom Joints

The top and bottom sections fit together like a box, with the step ensuring that the parts remain concentric. The greater the surface area you can glue, the better. Joint A is ideal for flatter tops. Taller vessels are best joined as in B. The flatness of the surface in C is difficult to check, as is the quality of the joint.

A   B   C

4. The blank for the body of the vessel is held by the top face on a screw chuck so that I can turn the profile. For roughing, I use shallow or half-round gouges, whose open shape lets the shavings fly clear more readily than the deep flute of bowl-hollowing tools. Be sure to keep a good diameter on the base—you'll need it for rechucking. Once the broad curve is developed, attend to the base and prepare for the next fixing.

5. I flatten the base by squeezing the gouge edge in with my upper hand for a scraping cut. Keep the tool rolled into the cut at 45°, as in the bottom photo on p. 121.

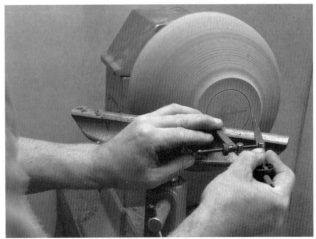

6. Lay out the foot diameter to fit your collet chuck. If you lack a chuck, a good alternative method here is to glue on a waste block and drill a center hole so the job can be remounted on a center-screw chuck.

8. The base is recessed to a depth greater than the flat at the top of the foot, which will be the base of the vessel. It is easier to recess the base now rather than later, when the nearly completed vessel will be held in a jam-fit chuck. Always do as much as possible while the job is held securely.

7. I like my ¼-in. (6mm) shallow gouge for cutting shoulders for the collet chuck; because catches don't really matter, I regard this step as a good opportunity to hone skills—the quality of finish is not important, since the foot will be turned away. A slight dovetail will fit better into the collet chuck.

9. Finish the profile, taking a back cut with a deep-fluted bowl gouge, using the steep inner edge of the tool. Do not try this using a shallow gouge. Get your body behind the tool for maximum control; tilt it just up from horizontal and point it in the direction you're cutting. In this position, the tool is easy to steer around the curve, provided you keep the bevel rubbing. If you move smoothly and evenly with the tool, you should cut a smooth and even curve. But the chances of doing it right the first time are remote, so this is where people get into trouble. If you get the projection of the curve you're cutting wrong, there are two basic scenarios, depending on its direction (see the drawings on the facing page).

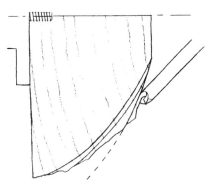

Scene one: You're cutting around the curve when you realize that you are not bringing the tool around fast enough and that the shaving is becoming thinner and thinner. Solution: Continue to take the tool on the same trajectory out into space. Then start to cut again from lower down the curve on a different trajectory. Never pivot the tool around to take a heavier shaving, because this usually ruins the curve, unless you are almost at the rim.

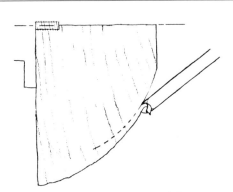

Scene two: You're cutting around the curve and taking an ever-heavier cut. Stop the moment you realize the situation, because you're going to have to change the basic form. Your options are these: recut to a shallower curve, recut to a smaller foot, or use the step for decoration or continue the curve but consider leaving a ring of material for beads. Don't sand at this stage because you might have to work on the profile again when the job is remounted.

10. Here I use a standard diamond-shaped parting tool to part off the bowl. For larger forms, I use the Stewart System slicer made by Sorbys (Sheffield, England), which is designed exactly for this task. It is stronger than the parting tool, which is only effective on blanks up to 8 in. (200mm) in diameter and 4 in. (100mm) deep. On soft woods, I have also used a 4-ft. (1220mm) length of 1-in. (25mm) by ¼-in. (9mm) flat-section steel ground and used like a parting tool, but the edge doesn't stay sharp for long. No matter what you use, you'll need to take several cuts to widen the kerf and allow the tool room to operate as the cut deepens. Maintain a firm grip on the tool to counteract catching and the tendency to twist, but you can reduce these problems by lowering lathe speed to 200 rpm to 400 rpm. Take care to line up the tool so that you don't go through the side or the base. I stop the lathe frequently to inspect the progress of the cut, and tap the bowl to see if it's loosening. It will usually start to wobble when the supporting material is down to about 2 in. (50mm), at which time a couple of taps should break it free. I used the inside of this blank for the top section of the lamp base on p. 159.

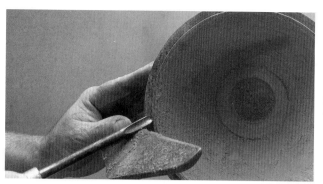

11. The base section is now remounted. First I use the ¼-in. (6mm) shallow gouge to turn a rabbet to match the one on the top. The bowl wall is flexible, so it needs support as I cut. I don't need any fingers on the center side of the tool, because the rotating wood wants to fling the tool away from the center. My thumb serves as the backstop to prevent kickback.

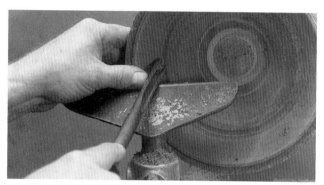

12. I use a similar grip to prevent chatter as I cut in from the rim to begin the final shaping of the inside. The ½-in. (13mm) deep-fluted gouge starts the cut rolled on its side with the top toward the center to avoid catches. Once the bevel is rubbing, it is rolled counterclockwise 45° to take a heavier shaving. As the cut proceeds deeper, chatter is less of a problem, so I can change my grip to exert more control on the fulcrum on the rest.

13. Use the lower portion of the edge to take a heavy cut, but don't overdo it and have a catch. It is usually more efficient to take two lighter cuts. If the shavings rapidly increase in size, stop the cut. Then pivot the tool back on the bevel shoulder and bring the edge in to take half the previous cut. Once the edge is in the wood, you can pivot the tool forward and have the bevel rubbing on the new cut. Take the wall thickness down to whatever you desire. I leave the wall at ¼ in. (6mm), maybe slightly less. Ultralightness seems pointless in a vessel designed primarily to grace the eye, although it does take on another dimension when handled.

14. The top is glued in place with the grain aligned as much as possible. I use cyanoacrylate glue or white glue, which is much slower to dry. The super glue allows you to carry straight on with the job. I turn the top flat using the small shallow gouge, then develop the detail around the opening.

15. I detail the joint with V-grooves. This confuses the eye with undulating grain patterns so that the joint is difficult to spot. If vibration is a problem, support the wood as you cut, sanding the surface first to reduce the friction and heat on your fingers.

16. I define the grooves further by using the skew chisel's long point very cautiously to cleave a line in the V-groove.

17. I found the flat top surface visually boring. Since this West Australian grasstree scrapes particularly well, I use a slightly curved scraper to turn a shallow curve. This needs a very delicate touch, with your hand supporting the vessel, but turning a top this thin makes a sound that discourages heavy cuts. A shearing cut with the small gouge and heavier sanding would be safer.

18. I refine the lower curve into the base, first using the arrowhead scraper, then the more acute angle of the small skew's long point to get in farther over the collet.

19. I prefer to use the angle drill for power sanding because it doesn't scud about like more conventional drills, which tend to kick sideways every time the disc touches the wood.

20. To complete the vessel, I mount it into a jam-fit carrier, with a waste pad to protect the base from the tail-center cone.

21. I fair the curve in to the base using my ¼-in. (6mm) shallow gouge, then sand it.

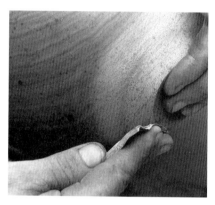

22. Finally, I back off the tail support and sand the base. I keep my hand pressed against the base at all times in case the vessel loosens in the carrier. You need to have your abrasives within easy reach at times like this.

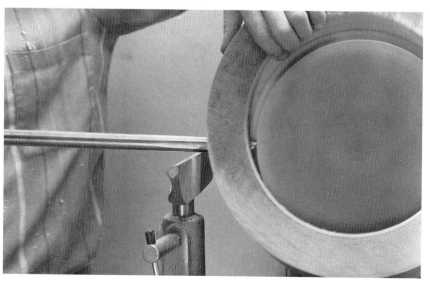

23. From the base section of a larger vessel I save several rings in lieu of shavings, which I can use later for inlay, picture or mirror frames, or for the table top shown on p. 143. I use a Stewart System slicer, designed primarily for nesting bowls, as shown on p. 155. In the drawing on the facing page you can see how much can be saved from blanks.

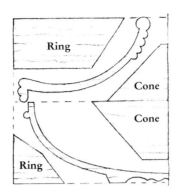

Design Variations

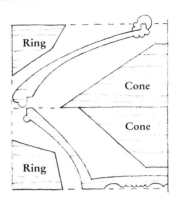

Lamp base made from three pieces, 11¾ in. (300mm) in diameter by 9½ in. (240mm) tall. Gilt varnish covers both joints while adding to the visual appeal of the whole. The top section came from the hollow form in the photo sequence on p. 155.

Bird nesting boxes. These are around 9 in. (230mm) in diameter, but you should check out the requirements of your local bird population with local ornithologists or specialist publications. A knot between each bead, as on the box at right, makes the tail hang better and with enough articulation for it to sway in a breeze. The beads on the box at left rest one upon another and look somewhat arthritic.

Ladles

Ladles, 1½ in. (38mm) in diameter
by 3¼ in. (85mm) long.

I always enjoy the fact that these ladles look laboriously carved, when in fact each is the product of a few minutes of turning and somewhat less time sanding. This makes them eminently suitable for production in a small workshop and an ideal cash-flow line for anyone setting up as a professional craft turner. The smaller ones always sell readily on their own (assuming the price isn't too outrageous) or as part of a bowl-and-scoop set.

I find it handy to keep scoops or ladles in every kitchen storage jar, so there are small ones in the spices, mid-size ones in the tea caddies and large ones in the rice and flour. I find this much better than having them out on display as decorative objects, always in sight and rarely appreciated. Hidden away in containers and ready for use, each trusty scoop lies in wait for me to renew and develop my acquaintance with its curves and details as I measure out the flour, dried fruit, cereal, rice or whatever. Why bother with an unattractive mass-produced plastic or metal equivalent?

You start to make a ladle by turning a sphere with a handle between centers. This is cut in half lengthwise to create two ladle blanks. The hemispherical ends are hollowed to form the ladle bowls, and finally a bit of carving refines the form by slimming the handle and rounding the top of both bowl and handle. You can see how the ladle shapes lie within the blanks in the drawing on p. 162. More dramatic shapes may be achieved by closing the angle between the bowl and handle as shown in B and C, but these waste most of the blank. As the bowl is hollowed, the handle protrudes from the chuck at 45°, which exposes your fingers during turning more than I consider comfortable. But there are those who regularly make scoops this way. You can see that it's the fan shape of the handle that lends charm to the design, and this can be accentuated by making the end of the rough handle even fatter. A ladle made on these lines with a straight handle is very prosaic.

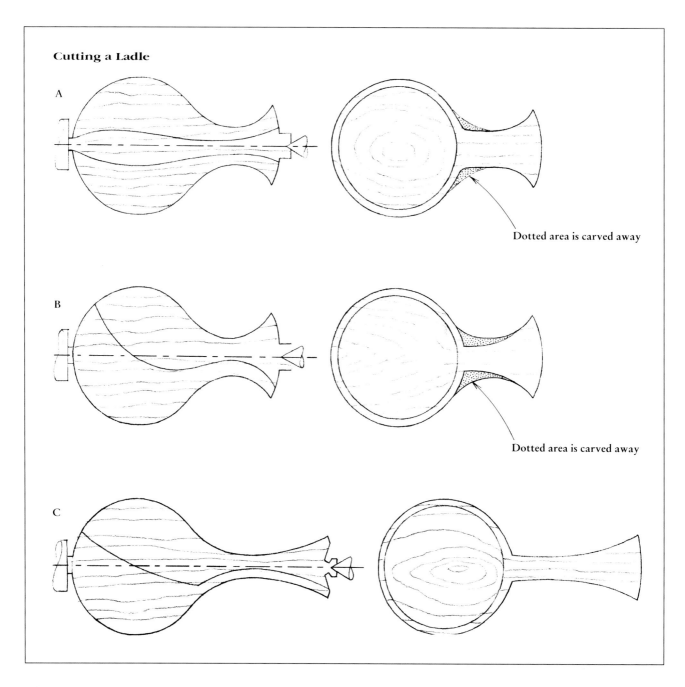

Cutting a Ladle

A

Dotted area is carved away

B

Dotted area is carved away

C

Cutting the initial turning in half to make two ladle blanks as shown at A can be hazardous to your fingers. Always push the handle through the bandsaw before the sphere and make sure that you cut down the center. I do this by eye, but you can support the blank in a V-carrier similar to the one shown on p. 143. If you push the spherical end through first, the initial pressure of the saw teeth on the sphere can snap the handle over into the blade, possibly with your fingers. Never attempt to use any sort of power saw to cut away the waste on the B-style or C-style ladles, where the cuts would be off-center. It is much safer, quicker and more accurate to turn the waste away on the lathe or use a disc sander as shown in step 11 in the photo sequence (see p. 166).

You can use just about any straight-grained length of wood for a ladle. A 2-in. (50mm) green branch is ideal. The pith will be cut away and the wood will shrink to leave you with an oval bowl and a ladle that looks anything but turned. Commercially, this means that in a few minutes you can make an object that looks as though it has taken hours to carve. Lathe speed should be between 1,800 rpm and 2,200 rpm.

Although the first stage of this project can be turned faster and more easily between centers, here I chose to mount the wood in a contracting collet chuck so that the sphere would be more visible; the spherical end fits into the chuck for the second fixing. If you want to work really fast and loose, turning random sizes, you can use a three-jaw chuck to grip different-diameter spheres, but there will be marks on the wood that must be hand-sanded away. Since I prefer to turn the sphere to fit a collet chuck, everything needs to be measured as work proceeds. Turners who make huge runs of something like this develop the useful knack of being able to turn a pretty good sphere by eye. The rest of us use templates made by drilling a hole the diameter of your sphere in a scrap of wood or metal, which is then cut in half. My standard ladle is 1⅝ in. (40mm) in diameter.

Turning a Ladle

1. Turn the blank true with the end grain flat, then turn at least 2 in. (50mm) of the end to fit your template.

2. Measure off a length equal to the diameter of the blank. Part in at right angles to the axis to establish the diameter of the sphere. Mark the center in pencil.

3. Turn the sphere, testing for roundness as you go by holding the template in various positions. Try to retain the pencil line to help you locate the center.

4. It is important to get the end round, since this will align with the hollow and affect the look of the rim. On the other side there is a margin for error—a bit of extra wood adds strength to the handle and is visually acceptable. But this side still needs to be fairly accurate to fit securely into the chuck.

5. After the handle is shaped and the job sanded, it's parted off, ready to be split into two ladle blanks. I cut back into the handle so there will be less waste to remove later.

6. Above left: This collet is a copy of the metal one supplied with the Precision Combination Chuck. If you are making only a few ladles, it's simpler to make a standard jam-fit chuck and cut a section of the rim away to accommodate the handle. When the blank is secured in the chuck, drill the depth hole. Clearly there is a hazard here because, with the center of the hemisphere set on the axis, the handle sticks out and rotates like a propeller.

7. Above right: Use a ¼-in. (6mm) deep-fluted gouge to hollow the bowl. Here I use the base of my little finger as the backstop and fulcrum. A clever photographic exposure reveals the position of the handle, as well as the collet jaws.

8. This is an alternative backstop grip using my third finger. Remember that this is facework and you are turning into cross grain here. Do not use the back-hollowing technique, which is strictly for hollowing end grain. I use a gouge with the bevel ground long on the left but near vertical on the right. This allows me to start the cut with the gouge rolled on its side, then rotate it onto the steeper bevel as the cut proceeds into the bottom of the bowl. Because I can keep the bevel rubbing, I can use a shearing cut to cut the curve in one sweep. With practice, the inside can be done in a few seconds, which makes the scoops a good production item.

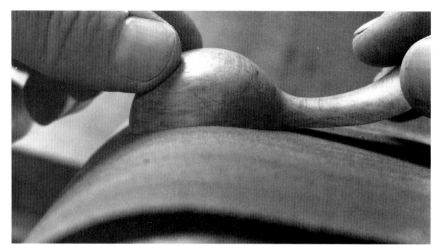

9. I use the belt sander to shape the top. It is at this stage that you can really start to impose your own character on the scoop as you refine the handle and top of the bowl.

10. Each of these scoops looks fine from the side after the initial sanding on the belt sander, with the curve of the handle sweeping down across the top of the bowl and then up to the rim. But from the top you can see the difference detailing can make to a handle.

11. You can whittle away the surplus material where the bowl meets the handle or use a sanding disc or small drum sander. Each way lends a different character and imposes a different style on the basic form. But be careful not to make the ladle too thin in the neck. Not only will it lack strength, but it will also look insubstantial and mean.

Design Variations

Caddy scoops; Simon Raffan, Lilydale, Tasmania, Australia.

These variations on the theme are all in constant use. Ladles at top: Simon Raffan, Lilydale, Tasmania, Australia; at bottom: Bonnie Klein, Seattle, Washington.

A dynamic variation full of vigor and presence; Terry Martin, Brisbane, Australia. Martin deliberately used a poor cutting technique to good advantage on the handle, which contrasts nicely with the smooth inside of the bowl.

Index

Page numbers in italics refer to photos and drawings.

168

Editor .... Laura Cehanowicz Tringali

Designer/layout artist .... Henry Roth

Copy/production editor .... Pam Purrone

Photographer .... Richard Raffan

Illustrator .... Lee Hochgraf Hov

Typeface .... ITC Garamond

Paper .... Warren Patina Matte, 70 lb., neutral pH

Printer and binder .... Arcata Graphics/Hawkins, New Canton, Tennessee

See Richard Raffan's turning projects on video.

BOOK/VIDEO SET

There's no better way to learn woodturning than by watching master turner Richard Raffan at the lathe. In his new video, Raffan demonstrates several projects from the book you're holding. You'll see the subtle movements, rhythms and flicks of the wrist that Raffan employs to create mallets, spatulas, hollow vessels and more. Throughout the tape Raffan explains what to do when things go wrong and provides the kind of gentle encouragement and inspiration that will get you headed for the shop and ready to turn. *90 minutes.*